The New

Shopping Guide

FACTORY OUTLETS AND WAREHOUSE SALES IN ONTARIO

As featured in the weekly columns
by **Cathie Mostowyk & Linda Sherman**
in The Toronto Star and Toronto Metro

CONTACT US

Shoestring Shopping Guide
Website:
www.shoestringshopping.com
www.toronto.com/shoestring
Fax: 416-236-4781

Cathie Mostowyk
President and Writer
Fax: 416-236-4781
e-mail:
shoestringshopping@rogers.com

Linda Sherman
Director of Sales and Writer
Tel: 416-232-0254
Fax: 416-232-9479
e-mail: lsherman@idirect.ca

Cybercom Publishing
Ben Harrison Publisher
Tel: 416-385-7973
Fax: 416-385-7974
e-mail: ben@cybercominc.net

Compiled by
CATHIE MOSTOWYK

Design, Layout & Production by Cybercom Publishing, Toronto, Ont. Canada
(416) 385-7973

Printed in Canada ISBN 0-9681404-7-5

A Personal Memo from

Cathie Mostowyk

(Author of The Shoestring Shopping Guide©)

Welcome to the world of "Shoestring 2003".

COVER STORY

This year's cover design is a reproduction of an original painting by Toronto artist Pat Ransom. Pat is a long time friend who shifted her career from the hi-tech industry to become a full time artist. We commissioned her to design this year's cover and wish her every success in the future.

BUSINESS LISTINGS

Businesses listed in the annual edition of The Shoestring Shopping Guide have been featured in the Shoestring column published each Monday in The Toronto Star and Toronto Metro. They do not pay for this listing. They are usually referred to us by our readers, have been visited and interviewed by my associate Linda Sherman or myself and finally, they have earned their inclusion in the column through consistently offering consumers a combination of quality and value that generally is not found elsewhere.

The publication of our annual edition each year is financed by advertising and book sales. This year, to keep "Shoestring" financially viable and eliminate redundancy, we have reduced the text write-up of businesses to include their name, address, telephone and internet addresses, plus warehouse sale information. We have also introduced a "Custom Listing" feature allowing businesses wishing to subscribe to this service, the opportunity to have an edited version of their weekly column included in the text write-up.

Please support these businesses as well as our advertisers. It is through their participation that we will be able to continue to bring you the Shoestring Shopping Guide Annual Edition in the years ahead.

FEEDBACK

We value your comments, constructive criticisms and of course, your referrals of your favourite places for value shopping. You may e-mail us at <shoestringshopping@rogers.com> or leave a message at 416-236-1489.

Best wishes from all of us at "Shoestring" to you and all the special people in your life.

Cathie Mostowyk.

table of contents

TIPS ON USING THE SHOESTRING SHOPPING GUIDE

Warehouse Sales: 🛍
Most of The Shoestring Shopping Guide columns which appear weekly in The Toronto Star and Toronto Metro are reproduced in our annual edition. Frequently the weekly columns feature warehouse sales and special events which may/may not be repeated annually. We have prepared a Warehouse Sale Calendar based on information we have available at the time of printing. These are indicated by a 🛍 sign following each business name, however it is always wise to call and confirm sale dates and location before starting out.

Advertisers:
Publication of the Shoestring Shopping Guide is made possible in part by the support of our advertisers. We ask you to reciprocate by supporting them and letting them know that you saw their listing/advertisement in Shoestring.

Colour advertisements are grouped in the center of the book, with specific page numbers displayed in their individual 'Text' write ups. Black and white ads are usually displayed out of the center section, close to their actual text write up.

The businesses listed with a descriptive text are either participating in our new 'Custom Listing' program or are new businesses that we have reported on during the past 12 months. All other businesses listed in Shoestring have appeared one or more times during previous years in our weekly Shoestring columns.

The Internet
The World Wide Web is playing an even bigger part in the business/consumer world than ever before. The Shoestring Shopping Guide columns may be accessed the week they are published on two web sites: www.toronto.com/shoestring and our own site, www.shoestringshopping.com. In addition you will also find 'links' to many of our advertiser's web sites.

table of contents

T.B.A. TO BE ANNOUNCED - DATES NOT AVAILABLE AT PRESS TIME

THIS SYMBOL INDICATES WARE-HOUSE SALES

GREY BOXES AROUND TEXT LISTINGS ARE VERY SPECIAL.
THEY REPRESENT OUR ADVERTISERS WITH CORRESPONDING PAGE NIMBERS TO THEIR ADVERTISEMENTS.

for your family

- **Family Wear**
- **Men's Wear**
- **Children's Fashions & Baby Needs**
- **Women's Fashions**
- **Footwear**
- **Bridal Fashions & Accessories**
- **Jewellery & Accessories**
- **Sportwear & Gear**
- **Personal & Healthcare Products**
- **Food Fair & Wine**

Ransom

family wear

A.S.I. CLOTHING COMPANY

You will find Great clothing here at Great Prices and in the latest styles, direct from the retailer's own local manufacturing plant using domestic fabrics and labour. They are able to pass considerable savings on to the consumer. Large stock selection of casual sportswear, active/dancewear, swimwear and outerwear in all departments, baby, youth, ladies and men's. Open year round with new product introductions ongoing along with popular name brands. Great for back-to-school and gift giving. Visa, MasterCard and Interac accepted. Also A.S.I. bonus points on purchases.

1224 Dundas St. (west of Dixie Rd.) Mississauga
Tel: 905-272-0813
Hours: M.-F. 10 a.m. to 9 p.m., Sat. 9 a.m. to 6 p.m., Sun. 11 a.m. to 5 p.m.
3245 Fairview St. Burlington (west of Walker's Line)
Tel: 905-681-2825.
Hours: M.-S. 10 a.m. to 6 p.m., Sun. 11 a.m. to 5 p.m.
Outlet store 2473 Dixie Rd. (south of Dundas St.) Mississauga
Tel: 905-272-1412.
Hours: Thurs. - Sun. 10 a.m. to 5 p.m.
Extended hours for Fall.

See advertisement on page A31

ASH CITY WAREHOUSE SALE

We found some great deals at this sale – particularly if you have a golfer on your Christmas list. This company sells logowear to corporate clients, so are clearing out their shirts, jackets, outerwear and fleece products. We found a great jacket for $30, and golf shirts are 2/$15. VISA and cash only.

2071 McCowan Road (north of Sheppard Ave.), Scarborough.
Tel: 416-292-6612
Hours: Call for 2002 sale dates and hours.

ATHLETIC SPORTS SHOW - EXERCISE AND BODYWEAR

2350 Cawthra Rd. (Q.E.W. to Cawthra Rd.), Mississauga.
Tel: 905-272-0813
Hours: M. to F. 9 - 6, Sat. 9 - 6, Sun. 12 - 5
Open 9-8 during Christmas season.

family wear

AU COTON DEPOT

Featuring a great selection of preshrunk, garment dyed ladies, men's and children's merchandise, this outlet is having an end of season manufacturer's seconds sale of up to 70% off regular prices. In addition, you'll find lots of in-store specials on regular items, prices starting from just $4.99. Mention Shoestring and receive 15% off your total purchase!

Warden Power Centre (Warden & St. Clair Avenue) Scarborough
Tel: 416-750-3037
Hours: Monday to Friday 10 a.m. to 9 p.m. Saturday 9:30 a.m. to 6 p.m.
Sunday noon to 5 p.m.

BARDEAUS FAMILY FASHIONS AND SPORTING GOODS CENTRE

We don't know of any other place where you can rent a tux, buy fishing gear, gut and wood frame snowshoes, better brand name clothing, jewellery, books, darts, souvenirs and a hundred and one other items in a store owned by one family for over eighty years and no it's not Eaton's. Semi annual clearances happen Feb./Mar. and Aug./Sept. with interesting ambiance and competitive everyday prices year round.

88 Sykes St., N., Meaford
Hours: Monday to Saturday 9-6, closed Sunday.

BLOWOUTS

We were skiing in Collingwood this past weekend, and dropped in to see this designer's clearance outlet en route. Now is a great time to visit as they have their "two for one" clearance sale with names that include Magnolia, Daiquiri, Kenneth Cole and some children's clothes as well. This outlet store always carries a wide variety of designer merchandise that changes often.

28 Bruce Street South (south off Hwy. 26), Thornbury
Tel: 519-599-5315
Hours: Mon. to Sat. 10 am to 5:30 pm, Sun. noon to 4 pm

CAMP CONNECTION GENERAL STORE

Lawrence Plaza, 526 Lawrence Ave. W. (northwest corner of Bathurst St. and Lawrence Ave.), Toronto
Tel: 416-789-1944
Hours: M to Fri 10:00 a.m. - 9:00 p.m.,
Sat 10:00 a.m. - 6:00 p.m., Sunday noon - 5:00 p.m.

CAULFEILD OUTLET STORE

Those of you heading north to cottage country can enjoy a break from driving, by stopping to save at the Barrie location. Past season's men's and ladies shirts, shorts, pants, sweaters, and jackets for golf by Izod Club and Cutter & Buck are offered at outlet store prices. As well, check out their great selection of Joe Boxer Mens & Girlfriend, and Caulfeild robes while you're there. There are also seconds and overruns. Savings of up to 80%.

> Downsview
> 1400 Whitehorse Rd. (Allen Rd. north past Sheppard Ave. to Steeprock).
> Tel: 416-636-5900
> Hours: M. to F. 10 - 5, Sat. 10 - 5
> Barrie
> 60 Bell Farm Rd. (exit Duckworth Ave. off Hwy. 400).
> Tel: 705-737-0743
> Hours: M. to F. 9:30 - 5, Sat. 10 - 4

See advertisement on page A4

CHOCKY'S

For over 40 years, Chocky's has stood as Toronto's best bet for name brand clothing at wholesale prices. Great buys on all your basic needs such as socks, underwear, rainwear, t-shirts from brand name manufacturers such as Calvin Klein, Elita, Jockey, Penmans, Gym Master, Hanes & Non Fiction. Whether it is Christmas, Back to School or Summer Camp, it's a true shopping paradise.

> 2584 Yonge Street (Chocky's on Yonge - north of Eglinton), Toronto.
> Hours: 7 days a week, call for hours
> Tel: 416-483-8227
> 327 Spadina Ave. (1-1/2 blocks north of Dundas St.), Toronto.
> Hours: 7 days a week, call for hours
> Tel: 416-977-1831

family wear

SUCHA DEAL

ENDS

NOW HAS THREE LOCATIONS

140 Avenue Rd.,
Toronto, Ontario
Tel: (416) 968-7272
Fax: (416) 968-7454

3376 Yonge Street
Toronto, Ontario
Tel: (416) 486-0591
Fax: (416) 486-2478

1930 Queen St. East
Toronto, Ontario
Tel: (416) 699-2271
Fax: (416) 699-5612

Since 1982, one of Toronto's original discounters
of clothing for women and men.

CLUB MONACO - OUTLET STORES
Colossus Centre 7575 Weston Rd.(at Hwy. 7) Woodbridge.
Tel: 905-265-0733
Hours: M. to F. 10 - 9, Sat. 9 - 6, Sun. 11 - 6
Call for other locations.

DANIER LEATHER FACTORY OUTLET
365 St. Clair Ave. W. Toronto
Toll free: 1-877-9DANIER
Hours: M-F 10 - 9; Sat. 9:30 - 6; Sun. noon to 5

EDDIE BAUER 🏬
If you're thinking new clothes for fall, this warehouse store is well stocked with fall clothing, as well as some spring and summer clearance merchandise. Their pricing policy is very simple - everything is 50% or more off the original ticketed price. You really can't beat that for quality Eddie Bauer clothing - Wheelchair accessible.
Real Eddie Bauer – Unreal Prices!!!
201 Aviva Park Drive (first lights north of Steeles Ave. off Weston Road), Vaughan.
Tel: 905 - 850-7016
Hours: M. to F. 10 - 7,
Sat. 10 - 6, Sun. 12 - 5

ENDS - CLEARANCE OUTLETS
Since 1982, ENDS has been one of Toronto's original discounters offering a constantly changing assortment of ladies and men's clothing. Discontinued and end-of-lines, liquidations and samples from all over the world in bins and on tables, give it all a party atmosphere. It not difficult to find designer wear at ridiculously low prices, buried among casual and outerwear selections.
140 Avenue Rd., (at Davenport Rd.), Toronto.
Tel: 416-968-7272
1930 Queen St. E., (east of Woodbine Ave.), Toronto.
Tel: 416-699-2271
New Store: 3376 Yonge St., Toronto
Tel: 416-486-0591

See advertisement on page 10

family wear

THE FACTORY STORE
41 Manitoba Street, Bracebridge.
Tel: 705-645-0355
Hours: M. to Sat. 9 - 6, Sun. 12 - 4 (Summer hours daily from 9 - 9)
Hours: Open 7 days a week year round.

GARY GURMUKH SALES LTD. 📇
179 Bartley Drive, Toronto.
Tel: 416-298-1610

HARPUR'S CLOTHING COMPANY LTD. - FACTORY OUTLET
2780 Dufferin St. (south of Lawrence Ave.), Toronto.
Tel: 416-781-2181
Hours: M. to F. 9 - 5

HILL STREET BLUES
Hill Street Blues carries just about all of the current branded men's and ladies
jeans, tops and bottoms, all priced at "Buy one get the second for half price."
The brands are well known names like Parasuco, Silver, Manager, Buffalo,
Guess, DKNY, Replay, Calvin Klein, Polo and Tommy Hilfiger. If you buy only
one pair of jeans, they'll even give you a "raincheck" for the second pair at
50% off for a future purchase. There are a couple of exceptions – Levis and
Replay are not included in the special pricing, as they are already well priced
(Levis are sold at everyday low price of $49.99).
Richmond Height Plaza,
10520 Yonge Street (approximately 1km north of Major Mackenzie),
Richmond Hill.
Tel: 905-737-3936
Hours: M. to F. 9:30 - 9, Sat. 9:30 - 6, Sun. 11 - 5

INTERNATIONAL - WAREHOUSE SUPERSTORES
111 Orfus Rd., North York.
Their locations are numerous so call for a location nearest to you.
Tel: 416-785-1771
Hours: M. to F. 9 - 9, Sat. 9 - 6, Sun. 10 - 5

JACK & PETER'S PLACE

This discount outlet is celebrating their 35th year of business in the same location. All their present and previous customers are invited to take advantage of super discounts of up to 70% off. Lots of tops, skirts, pants, suits, dresses, coats and more for men and women. Always great deals.

161 Spadina Ave. (south of Queen St.) Toronto,
416 971-5207
Hours: Monday to Saturday 8:30 a.m. to 5:30 p.m.

JUST DEALS

4490 Chesswood Drive, Unit 6, (between Dufferin and Keele Sts. south of Finch Ave.), Downsview.
Tel: 416-638-3862
Hours: M. to F. 9 - 5:30, Sat. 10:30 - 1:30

KETTLE CREEK OUTLET STORE

Clothing from previous seasons at 50 - 80% off. Lots of men's and women's denim jeans and cotton twill pants from $19.99, men's shirts and polos from $14.99 - $29.00, and women's sweater sets, skirts dresses and more at substantially reduced prices.

Six locations: For information please call their head office at
416-256-1145.

LE FIRME

Bursting at the seams with men's and women's designer fashions. The owners go direct to Italy and buy from Versace, Dolce , Gabbana, Ferre and Prada Sport. They also carry beautiful Christian Dior and J.P. Tods Bags.
95 East Beaver Creek, Unit 3, north off Hwy. 7 just east of Leslie St.), Richmond Hill.

Tel: 905 - 707-8727
Hours: M. to Sat. 11 - 6

LEVI'S OUTLET

Mississauga -Central Parkway Mall.
Tel: 905-270-7362
Call for other locations and hours. All locations open 7 days a week.

The New Shoestring Shopping Guide for 2003

LORNE'S FASHIONS
101 Spadina Avenue (at Adelaide St. W.)
Tel: 416-596-1058
Hours: M.-F.- 9-7; Sat. 9-6; Sun. 11-6.

MAGDER FURS
This is a great place to take your older furs to be updated, resized and restored. They will also reset buttons and retouch a collar. Gently used, but very wearable fur stoles from $99, and mink, muskrat and racoon coats from $199. Lots of new furs available at very reasonable prices also.
202 Spadina Avenue (at Dundas St. W.), Toronto
Tel: 416-504-6077.
Hours: M.T.W.- 9:30 – 6; Thur., Fri. 9:30 – 7; Sat. 9:30 – 6; Sun. 11 to 5.

MALABAR
Are little toes heading to a dance class? Point them in this direction & you'll find dance shoes, dance/exercise wear, accessories, theatrical makeup & more.
14 McCaul St. (just N. of Queen St. W.), Toronto.
Hours: M. to F. 9:30 - 6, Sat. 10 - 5
Tel: 416 -598-2581

MARKY'S WAREHOUSE OUTLET - OFF-PRICE STORE
7171 Yonge St. (at Doncaster Ave., just north of Steeles Ave.), Thornhill.
Tel: 905-731-4433
Hours: M. to F. 10 - 9, Sat. 10 - 6, Sun. 11 - 5

MILLWORKS FACTORY STORE
20 Bermondsey Rd., (just north of O'Connor Dr.), Toronto.
Tel: 416-285-6992
Hours: M. to F. 10 - 9, Sat. 10 - 6

Wear short sleeves! Support your right to bare arms!

family wear

McGREGOR SOCKS FACTORY OUTLETS

These outlets offer brand name socks and hosiery at up to 50% off - and have a pricing structure in place that lets you save more the more you buy. Brands include Calvin Klein, Levi's, GUESS, Dockers and popular McGregor brands like Weekender, Premium and Happyfoot. Great deals on irregular and discontinued items. Bring some friends and take advantage of bulk discounts. "Their prices will knock your socks off!"

> 30 Spadina Avenue, Toronto.
> Tel: 416-593-5353, ext. 344
> Hours: M.-Sat. 10-5
> 70 The East Mall at the Queensway.
> Tel: 416-252-3716, ext. 450
> Hours: Tues to Fri. 10-5.
> 1360 Birchmount Road (just north of Lawrence Ave.), Scarborough.
> Tel: 416-751-5511, ext. 528
> Hours: Tues. to Sat. 10-6; Sat 10-5

See advertisement on page A15

MUSKOKA LAKES WAREHOUSE SALE 🏠

Great clothing for both men and women at this sale which will feature cozy sweats, sweaters, fleece and other casual clothing items. Prices will range from 50-80% off retail, and they'll pay the GST. All sales final.

> 2345 Matheson Blvd. East, Mississauga (north of Eglinton Ave., and west of Renforth Road).
> Tel: 905 - 629-2829
> Hours: Call for sale dates and hours.

NEW YORK CLOTHING COMPANY

Cookstown Manufacturers Outlet Mall, (south east corner of Hwy. 400 and Hwy. 89), Cookstown.

> Tel: 705- 458-4190
> Hours: Regular mall hours are M. to F. 10-9 Sat., Sun. and holidays 9-6.

> ### To err is human, to moo bovine.

NORAMA DESIGN WAREHOUSE SALE 🏢
Great bargains on a wide assortment of fleece, jackets, mock turtles, t-shirts and lots more at prices of 50 to 70% off. All sportswear items are either discontinued or excess inventories - no seconds.

475 Fenmar Drive (north of Finch Ave., between Islington Ave. and Weston Rd.), North York.
Tel: 416-744-6994, ext. 212
Call for sale date and hours.

NORTHERN REFLECTIONS AND GETAWAY
Dixie Outlet Mall (Dixie Rd and Q.E.W.), Mississauga.
Tel: 905-278-9487
Hours: M. to F. 10 - 9, Sat. 9:30 - 6, Sun. 12 - 6

NOVITA FASHIONS
1668 Avenue Rd., Toronto.
Tel: 416-781-0673
Hours: M. to Sat. 10 - 6

ON THE FRINGE
3333 Lakeshore Blvd. W. (between Brown's Line and Kipling on south side), Etobicoke.
Tel: 416-255-1976
225 Main Street, Port Dover
Tel: 519-583-0023
Hours: M. & T. 10 - 6, W. to F. 10 - 7, Sat. 10 - 3. Call ahead first.

A good pun is its own reword.

THE PANTYHOSE SHOP

In September, The Pantyhose Shop will be celebrating 11 years in business providing great service, great products and great prices year round, to thousands of repeat customers. They carry the best selection of pantyhose in the city including brand names like Dim, Hue, Hanes. Wonderbra, Silks, Ibici, Ellen Tracy, Phantom, Givenchy, D.K.N.Y., Filodoro, Cafferena, Round The Clock, Berkshire and Nine West.

They also carry a great selecton of control and lifestyle undergarments like Flexees, Maidenform, Silks Under Control, Nancy Ganz, Cafferena, Bodywrap and the ever popular fine line of "Spanx: products. All goods are 1st. quality; no "deals", seconds or end-of-the-line merchandise.

> 136 Winges Rd., Unit 16 (south side of Hwy. 7 between Weston Rd. & Whitmore Dr. Woodbridge. (Look for the big black sign with "The Pantyhose Shop" in large yellow letters),
> Tel: 905-851-9929
> Hours: Mon. Tues. Wed. 9-6, Thur. Fri. 9- 7, Sat. 9 - 6

ROOTS CANADA LTD. - CLEARANCE CENTRES

> 1168 Caledonia Rd., North York.
> Tel: 905-501-1200
> Hours: M. to F. 10 - 9, Sat. 9:30 - 6, Sun. 12 - 5
> Call for other locations

SAMPLE SHOP

> 1093 Queen St. W. (at Dovercourt), Toronto.
> Tel: 416-534-3533
> Hours: M. to Sat. 10 - 4, Sun. 11 - 4

SHARC SALES - WAREHOUSE CLEARANCE

> 2 Essex Ave., Unit 4 (Bayview Ave. and Hwy. 7 area), Thornhill.
> Tel: 905-882-9840
> Hours: Call for hours.

SPARE PARTS CLOTHING OUTLET

> 59 Samor Road, Toronto.
> Tel: 416-781-2171
> Hours: Thu. - F. 11 - 7, Sat 11 - 6, Sun 11 - 5

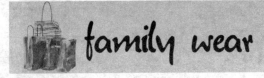

family wear

ST. MARCO IMPORTING
331 Trowers Rd., units 1 and 2 (south of Highway 7 and west of Weston Rd. Park in the back), Woodbridge.

   Tel: 905-850-0149

   Hours: M. to F. 9 - 5, Sat. 10 – 5

THE STOCKROOM
It's just one of those lucky finds for those who love tees and sweats. Brand name, first quality Fruit of the Loom and Gildan are all at great prices and the clearances on logo'd items are excellent. The 100% cotton t's are offered in over thirty colours with prices starting at $ 3.00 . Our teens especially liked the 15oz. hooded sweatshirt for $18.00 including taxes. The full line of Fruit of the Loom underwear is also available in men's and ladies styles. The sister company that shares the building, turns the product into promotional wear by doing screen printing and embroidery.

Cash, VISA, M/C

   115 Tycos Drive, (Dufferin & Lawrence) Toronto.

   Tel: 416 -785-5230

   Hours: M. to Thu. 8:30 - 4,

   F. 8:30 - 5, closed weekends.

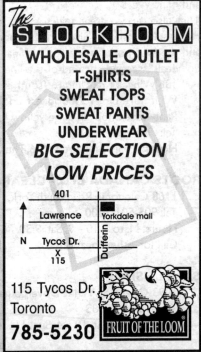

SUNNY CHOI OUTLET STORE
Many of you may be familiar with this Canadian designer's line of clothing. At this outlet store, you'll find suits, leisure wear, and a wonderful variety of evening wear. Inventory is mainly out of season and last year's lines, but the prices are 50 to 60% off regular prices.

   370 Steeles Ave. W., Unit 106 (one block west of Yonge Street), Thornhill

   Tel: 905-709-1678

   Hours: Monday to Friday 10 a.m. to 9 p.m., Saturday 10 a.m. to 6 p.m., Sunday noon to 5 p.m.

family wear

SUSSMAN'S - MEN'S AND LADIES WEAR 🛍
Junction Hwy. 6 and Hwy. 9, (main store is on the southeast corner, casual wear on the northwest corner and outlet store 1 block south on west side), Arthur.
Tel: 519-848-2660
Hours: M. to Thu. 9 - 6, F. 9 - 9, Sat. 9 - 6, Sun. 11 - 5; Outlet opens one hour later and closes one hour earlier.

TIGER BRAND KNITTING - FACTORY OUTLET
96 Grand Ave. S (across from Southworks Mall) Cambridge.
Tel: 519-624-7844
Hours: M. to W. 9:30 - 6, Thu. & F. 9:30 - 8, Sat. 9 - 6, Sun. 11 – 5

TILLEY ENDURABLES ANNUAL SECONDS SALE 🛍
Don't miss this annual Seconds Sale. The sale will consist of seconds and discontinued items discounted from 40% to 70%. A wide selection of Tilley Hats plus men's and women's pants, shorts, shirts, skirts, TilleyKnits, TilleySilks and Liberty of London prints will be available.
Location: To be announced.
Date: In early August for 2-3 weeks.
Tel: 416-444-6944. Call for 2003 dates, location, and hours.

TOM'S PLACE
Located in the heart of Kensington Market, Tom's Place is the premier location for the best selection of designer's quality men's and women's wear at below retail prices. With a selection of over 8,000 top brand name suits, this location has become the destination of the shopper with discriminating taste. Both men and women will be pleased with now expanded selection of business and casual clothing for every season or event. Featured in "The New York Times" and "American Airlines' magazine, Tom's Place is a one stop shopping experience for visitors to Toronto where on request, your purchases can be finely finished the same day.
190 Baldwin St. (between College St. & Dundas St., west off Spadina Ave. in the heart of Kensington Market) Toronto.
Tel: 416-596-0277
Website: www.toms-place.com
Hours: M. to W. 10-6, Thurs. & Fri. 10-7, Sat. 9-6, Sun. 12-5

See advertisement on page A9

---

family wear

UB WORLD FASHION OUTLET
55 Orfus Rd., (west off Dufferin St., north of Lawrence Ave.), North York.
Tel: 416-256-4777
Hours: Sat. to W. 10 - 6, Thu. & F. 10 - 8 Hours subject to change;
call first..

UNIVERSITY CLASS - FACTORY OUTLET
234 Hood Rd. (north of Steeles Ave., east of Warden Ave.), Markham.
Tel: 905-479-9929
Hours: M. to W. & Sat. 10 - 6, Thu. & F. 10 - 8, Sun. 12 - 5

URBAN BEHAVIOUR
Heartland Centre, (facing Britannia Rd., Between Mavis Rd. And
Rodeo Dr.), Mississauga.
Tel: 905-568-4121.
Hours: M. to F. 11-9, Sat. 10-6, Sun. 11-6.

THE OLDE HIDE HOUSE 🏠
If you have the winter blues, try a visit to this 30,000 sq. ft. store. Their Great
Canadian Coat Sale is on till January 21st at reductions anywhere from 15% to
50% off regular prices. Peruse their 30 room settings with values of 30% to
35% off until the end of January. They pride themselves on being the largest
leather store in Canada, using only top grain leather that will not leak colour.
Walk across the street also to their new warehouse that contains 100 pieces
of sofas, loveseats and chairs at even more significant savings.
49 Eastern Ave. Acton (401 west to Hwy. 25 at Milton, turn north
15 km. and follow signs).
Tel: 519-853-1031
Hours: 10 a.m. to 6 p.m. 7 days a week; Fri till 9 p.m.

THE WAREHOUSE - CLOTHING CLEARANCE CENTRE
574 Gordon Baker Rd. (south of Steeles Ave. E, west off of Victoria Park
Ave.), Scarborough.
Tel: 416-497-2659
Hours: M. to Sat. 11 - 6, Sun. 12 - 3:30

---

family wear

WEEKEND WARRIOR -
MANUFACTURER'S CLEARANCE OUTLET
210 Milner Ave., Units 5 & 6 (just off Markham Rd., north of the 401
Hwy.), Scarborough.
Tel: 416-297-1973
Hours: Thu. & F. 12 - 8, Sat. 10 - 6, Sun. 10 - 5

WINNERS
Winners offers 20%-60% savings on brand name and designer fashions for the
whole family, with a complete line of women's clothing and accessories
(including plus sizes and petites) as well as men's wear, junior fashions and children's wear. They also have a home fashion department offering great accessories for every room. Each store receives 10,000 new items weekly, so there
is always something new to discover.
60 locations across Ontario. Call for hours and location nearest you.
Tel: 1-877-WINN-877

Energizer Bunny arrested - charged with battery.

A man's home is his castle, in a manor of speaking.

men's wear

A.S.I. CLOTHING COMPANY

You will find Great clothing here at Great Prices and in the latest styles, direct from the retailer's own local manufacturing plant using domestic fabrics and labour. They are able to pass considerable savings on to the consumer. Large stock selection of casual sportswear, active/dancewear, swimwear and outer-wear in all departments, baby, youth, ladies and men's. Open year round with new product introductions ongoing along with popular name brands. Great for back-to-school and gift giving. Visa, MasterCard and Interac accepted. Also A.S.I. bonus points on purchases.

    1224 Dundas St. (west of Dixie Rd.) Mississauga
    Tel: 905-272-0813
    Hours: M.-F. 10 a.m. to 9 p.m., Sat. 9 a.m. to 6 p.m., Sun. 11 a.m. to 5 p.m.
    3245 Fairview St. Burlington (west of Walker's Line)
    Tel: 905-681-2825.
    Hours: M.-S. 10 a.m. to 6 p.m., Sat. 10 a.m. to 6 p.m., Sun. 11 a.m. to 5 p.m.
    Outlet store 2473 Dixie Rd. (south of Dundas St.) Mississauga
    Tel: 905-272-1412.
    Hours: Thurs. - Sun. 10 a.m. to 5 p.m.
    Extended hours for Fall.   See advertisement on page A31

CAULFEILD OUTLET STORE

Both the Downsview and the Barrie outlet stores are full of end-of-line men's and ladies golfwear and sportswear at up to 80% off. They have a huge selection of clearance lines like Izod Club, Cutter, Buck and Joe Boxer, Caulfeild men's robes and more. You will also find samples and seconds at great prices year round.

    Downsview: 1400 Whitehorse Rd. (Allen Rd. north of Sheppard Ave. to
    Steeprock Dr.),
    Tel: 416-636-5900
    Hours: M.-F. 10-5; Sat. 10 - 4
    Barrie: 60 Bellfarm Rd. (Duckworth exit from Hwy. #400)
    Tel: 705-737-0743
    Hours: M.-F. 9:30-5; Sat. 10-4

        See advertisement on page A4

A pessimist's blood type is always b-negative.

---

men's wear

CHRISTIAN DAVID
If the man in your life has a wedding looming, drop into this outlet offering formal and dress shirts for $19.95. Pick up a black bow tie with a shirt for only $6! All of their Wenger Swiss Army Knives and watches are also on sale until Father's Day at 30% off. Other interesting items for men also available, and check out their large smoking lounge and Cigar Club while you're there!

9 Advance Road, 2nd floor
(south of Bloor St., west off Islington Ave.), Toronto
Tel: 416-232-9876
Hours: Monday to Friday, 10:30 a.m. to 8 p.m., Saturday 10 a.m. to 6 p.m. Closed Sunday.

FORSYTHE FACTORY STORES
Cookstown Manufacturer's Outlet Mall, Unit 9B, Cookstown.
Tel: 705- 458-0436
Hours: M. to F. 10 - 9, Sat. & Sun. 9 - 6, holidays 9 - 6

FREEMAN FORMAL WEAR - WAREHOUSE SALE 🗄
Tuxedos previously used in their rental stock are being sold from $99 up. Formal shirts are $9.99. Also a large selection of used accessories at low prices. Sale on while inventory lasts. Warehouse sale in October, call for details

111 Bermondsey Rd., north entrance, (east of the Don Valley Parkway, south of Eglinton Ave.), Toronto.
Tel: 416-288-1919
Hours: M. to F. 9 - 9, Sat. 9 - 5, Sun. 12 - 5

GREG NORMAN OUTLET
Cookstown Manufacturers Outlet Mall, (south east corner of Hwy. 400 and Hwy. 89), Cookstown.
Tel: 705- 458-7097
Hours: Mall hours are M.-F. 10-9; Sat, Sun., Holidays, 12-5.

HARRY ROSEN MENSWEAR OUTLET STORE
Heartland Centre. Hwy 401 and Hurontario Street (west on Brittania Road.), Mississauga.
Tel: 905-890-3100
Hours: M.-F. 10-9; Sat. 9-6; and Sun. 11-5.

men's wear

HATHAWAY FACTORY STORE
707 St. Lawrence St. (east on Hwy. 401 to the Edward St./Prescott exit, south on Edward, right on Wood St., follow Wood St. to St. Lawrence St. and turn right), Prescott.
Tel: 613-925-5965
Hours: M. to F. 9:30 - 4:30, Sat. 9 - 4

JACK FRASER - MENSWEAR OUTLET STORE
Six locations, call for information.
Tel: 416-780-2150
Hours: M. to Sat. 9:30 - 6, Sun. 12 – 5

justwhiteshirts.com
In the mid nineties, three Canadian professionals, recognizing a personal need, started an on-line company to manufacture and sell high quality 100% cotton white shirts and black socks. Today they ship across North America and offer an enhanced line from Tuxedos to Weekend Casual Wear including a JWS Twill Shirt, a Mock Turtleneck and a new Polo Style knit. Our publisher, Ben dropped into an advertised sale at their Leslie/401 location, bought 3 shirts at great prices and said, "Our readers have got to hear about this place." They have an annual Christmas sale and are considering repeating the just completed Summer sale. They have an excellent e-commerce web site www.justwhiteshirts.com for on-line shopping.
Company Store: 1991 Leslie Street, Toronto
Tel: 1-800-221-8595
Call for hours and sale date(s)

KORRY'S CLOTHIERS
A high quality men's wear store that has been servicing men in southern Ontario for 50 years. Now is the time to visit and pick up some real bargains to update your wardrobe during their January sale. Italian fabric, Canadian made suits are always two for the price of one, but this month, designer suits are half price, along with sport shirts, knit sweaters, top coats and leather jackets.
569 Danforth Ave., (west of Pape Ave. on south side) Toronto.
Tel: 416-463-1115.
Hours: Monday to Wednesday 9:30 a.m. to 6:30 p.m., Thursday and Friday 9:30 a.m. to 9 p.m., Saturday 9 a.m. to 6 p.m.

men's wear

MILLENIUM 🏠

The space may get crowded with buyers but with savings of 50 to 70% off retail prices on samples, and ends of lines of quality men's and ladies wear, it should be worth checking out. No credit cards. April and November Warehouse Sales.

    72 Wingold Ave., Toronto.
    Tel: 416-703-3988
    Hours: W. Thu. F., noon-8; Sat. 10-6; Sun. noon-5.

MOORES MENSWEAR 🏠

Clearance centres: We are often asked why there aren't more menswear clearance centres, so just for you, Moores has two locations. Savings of up to 70% on a variety of discontinued and end-of-line menswear including suits, sport jackets, ties, shirts etc. make this a spot to check out for the man in your life.

    129 Carlingview Dr. (Carlingview exit off Highway 401 West) Etobicoke.
    Tel: 416-675-1900
    Hours: M.- T. 9:30 - 6, W. to F. 9:30 - 9, Sat. 9:30 - 5, Sun. 10:30 - 5
    3711 Lawrence Ave. E. (east of Markham Rd.), Scarborough.
    Tel: 416-675-1900 (CAll for sale date(s).
    Hours: M. to T. 9:30 – 6; W. to F. 9:30 - 9; Sat. 9 - 6; Sun. 11 - 5.

See advertisement on page 26

RIDOLFI SHIRTMAKER INC. - FACTORY SHOWROOM

    2901 Steeles Ave. W. #19 (southeast corner at Keele St.), Downsview.
    Tel: 416-667-0028
    Hours: M. to F. 9 - 5, Sat. 10 - 3
                                🏠

ROYAL SHIRT COMPANY LTD. $

    40 Addesso Drive (just east of Hwy. 400 and north of Steeles Ave.),
    Concord.
    Tel: 905-738-4676
    Hours: Call for specific dates and times.

A hangover is the wrath of grapes.

MOORES
Clearance Centre

GREAT QUALITY! LOW PRICES!

Savings of up to 70% off our Everyday Low Prices!

Suits	from $100	*Shoes*	from $29⁹⁹
Sportcoats	from $45	*Casual Pants*	from $15⁰⁰
Dress Pants	from $30	*Dress Shirts*	from $7⁹⁹

ONE LOCATION ONLY!
129 CARLINGVIEW DR.
ETOBICOKE
TEL. 416-675-1900

Moores
CLOTHING FOR MEN
Well Made. Well Priced. Well Dressed.

STORE HOURS: *MONDAY:* 9:30 AM TO 7:00 PM   *TUESDAY – FRIDAY:* 9:30 AM TO 9:00 PM
SATURDAY: 9:00 AM TO 6:00 PM   *SUNDAY:* 11:00 AM TO 5:00 PM

ALL MAJOR CREDIT CARDS ACCEPTED • PANT HEMMING AVAILABLE WHILE YOU WAIT
ALTERATIONS DONE ON PREMISES

men's wear

STOLLERY'S 💲

Established since 1901, this store is an icon on the corner of Bloor and Yonge where my father and grandfather shopped. They have over 30,000 sq. ft. on four levels of men and women's clothing. This month, there are lots of selected special items throughout the store from 20% to 70%. Great buys for ladies on their jackets with a skirt or pants regularly $610, now $299. Men's suits, sweaters, coats and ties all on sale along with their fancy dress shirts.

    1 Bloor St., Toronto 416-922-6173

    Hours: Monday, M., T., W. 9:30 a.m. to 7:00 p.m., Thu. and Fri. till 9:00 p.m., Sat. 9:30 a.m. to 6 p.m. and Sun. noon to 5 p.m.

THE SUIT EXCHANGE

    55 Orfus Road (west off Dufferin Street, north of Lawrence Ave.), Toronto.

    Tel: 416-782-4900

    Hours: M. to F. 11 - 9, Sat. 10 - 6, Sun. 11 - 6

TIMBERLAND - OUTLET STORE

    Heartland Centre, (just east off Mavis Rd. between Britannia Rd. W and Matheson Blvd.), Mississauga. Tel: 905-507-0004

    Hours: M. to F. 9:30 - 9, Sat. 9:30 - 6, Sun. 11-5.

TOM'S PLACE 💲

Located in the heart of Kensington Market, Tom's Place is the premier location for the best selection of designer's quality men's and women's wear at below retail prices. With a selection of over 8,000 top brand name suits, this location has become the destination of the shopper with discriminating taste. Both men and women will be pleased with now expanded selection of business and casual clothing for every season or event. Featured in "The New York Times" and "American Airlines" magazine, Tom's Place is a one stop shopping experience for visitors to Toronto where on request, your purchases can be finely finished the same day.

    190 Baldwin St. (between College St. & Dundas St., west off Spadina Ave. in the heart of Kensington Market) Toronto.

    Tel: 416-596-0257

    Website: www.toms-place.com

    Hours: M. to W. 10-6, Thurs. & Fri. 10-7, Sat. 9-6, Sun. 12-5

See advertisement on page A9

# men's wear

TUXEDO ROYALE WAREHOUSE SALE 🏛

We have at least two black tie events looming shortly, and with the holiday season approaching, I'm sure many of you do as well. This sale will include new wool tuxedos from $199, previously enjoyed tuxedos from $99, formal shirts from $29, and all of the tuxedo accessories that really make the man!

185 Konrad Crescent (south of Hwy 7, west of Woodbine Avenue), Markham.

Tel: 416-798-7617

Hours: Call for date and time of sale.

My wife really likes to make pottery,
but to me it's just kiln time.

Dijon vu - the same mustard as before.

Practice safe eating - always use condiments.

---

children's fashion and baby needs

A.S.I. CLOTHING COMPANY

You will find Great clothing here at Great Prices and in the latest styles, direct from the retailer's own local manufacturing plant using domestic fabrics and labour. They are able to pass considerable savings on to the consumer. Large stock selection of casual sportswear, active/dancewear, swimwear and outer-wear in all departments, baby, youth, ladies and men's. Open year round with new product introductions ongoing along with popular name brands. Great for back-to-school and gift giving. Visa, MasterCard and Interac accepted. Also A.S.I. bonus points on purchases.

 1224 Dundas St. (west of Dixie Rd.) Mississauga
 Tel: 905-272-0813
 Hours: M.-F. 10 a.m. to 9 p.m., Sat. 9 a.m. to 6 p.m., Sun. 11 a.m. to 5 p.m.
 3245 Fairview St. Burlington (west of Walker's Line)
 Tel: 905-681-2825.
 Hours: M.-S. 10 a.m. to 6 p.m., Sun. 11 a.m. to 5 p.m.
 Outlet store 2473 Dixie Rd. (south of Dundas St.) Mississauga
 Tel: 905-272-1412.
 Hours: Thurs. - Sun. 10 a.m. to 5 p.m.
 Extended hours for Fall.

See advertisement on page A31

BABY PLUS AND BUNKS 'N' BEDS

 14 Cedar Pointe Dr., Building 4A (Hwy. 90 exit, first street west of
 Hwy. 400), Barrie.
 Tel: 705-734-9356
 Hours: M. T. & Sat. 9 - 6, W. to F. 9 - 9, Sun. 11 - 5

BEAUTY INDUSTRIES - MILL OUTLET

 270 Sherman Ave. N. (north off Barton St. E., just past the train
 tracks), Hamilton.
 Tel: 905-549-1357
 Hours: M. to Sat. 10 - 5

Did Noah keep his bees in archives?

---

children's fashion and baby needs

CRAWFORD BOYS 🛍

Crawford Boys is Toronto's only store which specializes in dress and upscale casual clothing for boys ages 4-16. Sizes range from 4-20 as well as hard to fit HUSKY sizes 10-22. Suits, sports jackets, dress/casual pants and shirts etc. Designers names such as Perry Ellis, Givenchy, Hilfiger, Nautica and Guy La Roche. Professional, friendly staff. Alterations done on the premises.

> 508A Lawrence Ave. W (Lawrence Plaza – N.W. corner of Lawrence Ave. at Bathurst.), Toronto.
> Tel: 416-782-8137
> Fax: 415-916-5127
> e-mail: crawfordboys@hotmail.com
> Hours: Call for sale dates and hours.

DAN HOWARD'S MATERNITY - FACTORY OUTLETS

This store is a marvelous spot for maternity clothes. Fall and winter merchandise is being cleared now and is exceptionally well-priced.

> 257 Dundas St. E., (between Cawthra Rd. & Hwy. 10), Mississauga.
> Hours: M. & Thu. 10 - 9, T., W., F. & Sat. 10 - 6, Sun. 12 - 5
> Tel: 905 - 848-6776
> 300 Steeles Ave. W. (in Toys 'R' Us Plaza), Thornhill.
> Hours: M. & Thu. 10 - 9, T., W., F. & Sat. 10 - 6, Sun. 12 - 5
> Tel: 905 - 731-6177

DEAR-BORN BABY EXPRESS

This shop continues to offer great value for all your baby needs at very competitive prices. Right now, it has a large selection of winter clearance items at savings of up to 70%, as well as custom crib linen at 50% off. It is an authorized dealer for Perego, Moriguean, Lepine, Evenflo, Graco and many more. Ask about the photography service while you're there.

> 72 Doncaster Ave. (one light north of Steeles Ave.), Thornhill.
> Tel: 905-881-3334
> Hours: M. to W. & Sat. 10 - 6, Thu. & F. 10 - 9, Sun. 12 - 5

DIAPERS ETC. - FACTORY OUTLET

> 734 Kipling Ave., Toronto.
> Tel: 416-503-0313
> Hours: M. to F. 10 - 8, Sat. 10 - 6, Sun. 10 - 5
> Call for other locations.

children's fashion and baby needs

FAIRLAND
241 Augusta Ave. (Kensington Market area), Toronto.
Tel: 416-593-9750
Hours: M. to Sat. 9 - 7, Sun. 12 - 5

JACADI CHILDREN
Exclusive French label children's shops are celebrating their 10th Anniversary with a month long 40% off sale of all 2002 spring and summer collections of baby and children's clothing, shoes and accessories. At these discounts, go early, as selections won't last long. All sales are final.

Hazelton Lanes Shopping Centre, 87 Avenue Rd., (north of Bloor St., free 1 _ hour parking with purchase).
Tel: 416-923-1717.
Bayview Village Shopping Centre, 2901 Bayview Ave. (at Sheppard Ave. E.)
Tel: 416-733-1717
Hours: Monday to Friday 10 a.m. to 9 p.m., Saturday 10 a.m. to 6 p.m., Sunday noon to 5 p.m.

JACK RABBITS CLOTHING COMPANY
Evolving out of their home-party based business, this Canadian manufacturer of quality children's clothing is now sold through five on-going outlets. Sizes range from 12 months to pre-teen with savings of 20 - 60% off regular pricing now available year round.

132 St. George St., Brantford.
Tel: 519- 751-4791
Hours: M. to F. 10 - 5:30, Sat. 10 - 5
Cookstown Manufacturers Outlet Mall, RR#1, 3311 Hwy. 89, Cookstown.
Tel: 705- 458-2512
Hours: Regular Mall Hours.
1105 Wellington Road, London
Tel: 519- 622-6111
Hours: Regular Mall Hours.
Southworks Outlet Mall, 64 Grand Avenue S., Cambridge.
Tel: 519- 686-9462
Hours: Regular Mall Hours

children's fashion and baby needs

KID'S COSY COTTONS - FACTORY OUTLET

2620 Lancaster Rd. (opposite the Tommy and Lefebvre Sale), Ottawa.
Tel: 613- 523-2679
Hours: M. to F. 10 - 4
Call for sale dates.

KIDS ONLY CLOTHING CLUB WAREHOUSE SALE 🛍

After 14 years of home parties, Kids Only Clothing is closing and having a
huge warehouse sale. Over 100,000 pieces of babies, kids, and ladies clothing
items at 50% off the regular retail prices. You will also find a limited selection
of accessories such as socks, scrunchies, hair bands and hats. Items arrive
weekly, so shop often.

6991 Millcreek Drive, Unit 11, at Derry Road, Mississauga (just a short
distance from Erin Mills Parkway/Mississauga Rd. exit of Hwy. #401.
Tel 905 - 858-8500.
Hours: Now to mid-October, Monday to Friday 10 a.m. to 8 p.m.,
Saturdays 10 a.m. to 6 p.m., Sunday 10 a.m. to 5 p.m.

MISSISSAUGA PARENTS OF MULTIPLE BIRTHS ASSOCIATION

We occasionally let you know about these sales that periodically happen
throughout the GTA as well as other areas of Canada. This particular sale
includes as many as 70 families of twins and triplets who sell their maternity
and baby items. A great spot if you have a growing family as there are tons of
good deals.

If you are interested in finding out about other sales, please call the
national office at 905-888-0725.
Tel: 905-812-1797

PLUMLOCO CLOTHING COMPANY

114 Mississauga St. E., Orillia.
Tel: 705-325-1419
Hours: M. to Thu. 10 - 6, F. 10 - 9, Sat 10 - 6, Sun 10 - 5.
Call for other locations and hours

**I fired my masseuse today.
She just rubbed me the wrong way.**

---

children's fashion and baby needs

RAN'S MATERNITY WAREHOUSE SALE 🎁

You will always find bargains at Ran's Maternity. They are open year round and carry business, formal and casual maternity wear. Sales featuring seasonal merchandise ranging from 30-70% off occur in April and October. Great staff to assist you.

> 20 Maud St., Suite 401 (west of Spadina between Richmond and Adelaide St.) Toronto
> Tel: 416 703-1744
> Hours: Tuesday to Friday 11-6 p.m. Call for evenings and weekend hours.

SIBLINGS

This niche retailer specializes in fashions for girls aged 7 to 16. They are predicting that vintage-looking denim; faux suede tops and velour joggers will be the hot items for Fall.

They are holding a back-to-school sale with all their hot new items featuring buy one item and get the second half price. Start your school shopping early and pick up some bargains here at the same time.

> 107 Orfus Rd. (south of Hwy. #401 at Dufferin St.) Toronto.
> Tel: 416-256-7779.
> Hours: Sunday August 11 to September 3, Sunday to Wednesday 10 a.m. to 6 p.m., Thursday and Friday 10 a.m. to 9 p.m., Saturday 10 a.m. to 6 p.m.

SNUGABYE FACTORY OUTLET

Who doesn't have at least one small person on their Christmas list? This outlet sells great quality baby clothing. If you have small children of your own, you'll love the good selection of sleepwear, underwear, playwear, hosiery and bedding at prices that are at least 40% off retail.

> 188 Bentworth Avenue (corner of Caledonia Road), Toronto.
> Tel: 416-783-0300
> Hours: M. -Sat. 10-5.

See advertisement on page A30

A Freudian slip is when you say one thing but mean your mother.

SNUG AS A BUG

New for spring is an entire new line of clothing all bearing the "best value" label, which is priced at approximately 25% lower than regular price. We were especially pleased to find good sun hats for children available in a wide selection of sizes, prints and solids for both boys and girls. These are all with a safe chinstrap and up to 35% off. Sizes here range from newborn to six years. Refreshments and movies for the kids as you shop.

91 Brandon Ave., (off Dufferin Street between Dupont and Davenport Road), Toronto Tel: 416-534-6881

Hours: Call for sale dates and hours.

SODAPOP

315 Roncesvales Avenue (approximately 5 blocks south of Bloor).

Tel: 416-516-4200

Hours: T. W. 10-6; Th. Fri. 10-8; Sat. 10-6, Sun. 11-5.

TEDDY BEAR DIAPER SERVICE - FACTORY OUTLET

The company offers a cloth diaper service, but has a small outlet offering bargains on related items, such as pool pants, maternity/ nursing products. Cash or Visa accepted.

246 Brockport Dr., Unit 27 (west of Hwy. 27 and north off Belfield Rd.), Etobicoke.

Tel: 416-798-2328

Hours: M. to F. 9 - 4:30

WEEBODIES FACTORY STORE

481 North Service Road West, Suite A31 (exit at Dorval Road; between Dorval Road and 4th Line Road, Oakville.

Tel: 905-827-7004

Hours: Tues. to Sat. 10 - 5

I used to work in a blanket factory, but it folded.

ANNA THE FASHION OUTLET

2399 Cawthra Rd., Unit 24-25, (east side, north of the Queensway), Mississauga.
Tel: 905-896-0807
Hours: M. to F. 9-5:30; W. 9-7; Sat.: 10-3:30.

A.S.I. CLOTHING COMPANY

You will find Great clothing here at Great Prices and in the latest styles, direct from the retailer's own local manufacturing plant using domestic fabrics and labour. They are able to pass considerable savings on to the consumer. Large stock selection of casual sportswear, active/dancewear, swimwear and outer-wear in all departments, baby, youth, ladies and men's. Open year round with new product introductions ongoing along with popular name brands. Great for back-to-school and gift giving. Visa, MasterCard and Interac accepted. Also A.S.I. bonus points on purchases.

1224 Dundas St. (west of Dixie Rd.) Mississauga
Tel: 905-272-0813
Hours: M.-F. 10 a.m. to 9 p.m., Sat. 9 a.m. to 6 p.m., Sun. 11 a.m. to 5 p.m.
3245 Fairview St. Burlington (west of Walker's Line).
Tel: 905-681-2825.
Hours: M.-S. 10 a.m. to 6 p.m., Sun. 11 a.m. to 5 p.m.
Outlet store 2473 Dixie Rd. (south of Dundas St.) Mississauga
Tel: 905-272-1412.
Hours: Thurs. - Sun. 10 a.m. to 5 p.m.
Extended hours for Fall.   See advertisement on page A31

AU COTON DEPOT 🏠

Featuring a great selection of preshrunk, garment dyed ladies, men's and children's merchandise, this outlet is having an end of season manufacturer's seconds sale of up to 70% off regular prices. In addition, you'll find lots of in-store specials on regular items, prices starting from just $4.99. Mention Shoestring and receive 15% off your total purchase!

3 Brentwood Rd. North (west of Royal York, north of Bloor) Etobicoke.
Tel: 416-239-0559; Fax: 766-0386
Hours: T.-F. 10-6; Sat. 10 - 5:30.

women's fashion

BARB'S FASHION OUTLET 🏠
257 Main Street East, Stayner.
Tel: 705-428-3977
Hours: M. to Sat. 9:30 - 5:30, F. 9:30 - 9, Sun. 12 – 4
Summer hours: Sun. 12 - 4; open Sun. in December - 12 - 4

BLUE BAYOU FACTORY OUTLET
88 Doncaster Ave., (east off Yonge St., north of Steeles Ave.), Thornhill.
Tel: 905-771-9159
Hours: M. to W. & Sat. 9:30 - 6, Thu. & F. 9:30 - 9, Sun. 12 - 5

COLOURS EXCHANGE 🏠
Celebrating its 20th year in business, Colours Exchange is a terrific consignment shop; a favourite for anyone looking for quality in previously owned ladies wear. Great selection of women's designer and high quality clothing, shoes and accessories. Prices are slashed even more during the off-season. Appointments can be arranged to bring in items for resale. New arrivals daily.
3 Brentwood Rd. North (west of Royal York, north of Bloor) Etobicoke.
Tel: 416-239-0559; Fax: 766-0386
Hours: T.-F. 10-6; Sat. 10 - 5:30.

See advertisement on page A10

COTTON GINNY – POWER CENTRES OUTLETS
Brockington Plaza, 1725 Kingston Rd., Pickering.
Tel: 905-686-3035
Hours: M. to F. 10 - 9, Sat. 9:30 - 6, Sun. 12 - 5
Call for other locations and hours.

DAN HOWARD'S MATERNITY - FACTORY OUTLETS
300 Steeles Ave. W. (in Toys 'R' Us Plaza), Thornhill.
Tel: 905-848-6776
Hours: M. & Thu. 10 - 9, T., W., F. & Sat. 10 - 6, Sun. 12 - 5

I used to be a lumberjack, but I just couldn't hack it, so they gave me the axe.

DANYA FASHION SHOPPE 🏺

This is another amazing ladies high-end store sale that is not to be missed. Fall day and evening collections of Ellen Tracy, Eileen Fisher, Ann Klein, Olsen, Jones and more all on sale at up to 50% or more. Their sportswear, coats, jackets and will be on sale till February.

2378 Bloor St. W. (Bloor West Village, one and a half blocks east of Jane St.), Toronto.
Tel: 416-766-4511
Hours: M.-S. 10-6;. (Tue. & Fri. to 8); Sun noon to 5.

DESIGNER FASHION EMPORIO

"Discover..."Designer Fashion Emporio"...you'll be glad you did. Ladies designer fashions for less every day! Labels like Della Spiga and Mario Serrani at factory prices, directly to you! Take advantage of their everyday low prices on great quality designer fashions. Start the season right, come in the early fall months to take advantage of their special promotion of 50-70% off the entire new fall 2002 collections."

NORTH:	Woodbridge 100 Marycroft Ave. Unit 1
	Tel: 905.856.7199
Markham:	330 Esna Park Drive, Unit 38
	Tel: 905.415.3768
CENTRAL:	Toronto 1375 Yonge St.
	Tel: 416-921-1813
	Toronto 2587 Yonge St.
	Tel: 416-440-0079
WEST:	Mississauga 30 Eglinton Ave. W.
	Tel: 905-890-5840
BURLINGTON:	3480 Fairview St.
	Tel: 905-681-6103

Hours: Monday to Wednesday 10 a.m. to 5 p.m., Thursday and Friday 10 a.m. to 7 p.m., Saturday 10 a.m. to 5 p.m., Sunday noon to 5 p.m

See advertisement on page A3

EDDIE BAUER 🏺

If you're thinking new clothes for fall, this outlet store is well stocked with fall clothing, as well as some spring and summer clearance merchandise. Their pricing policy is very simple - everything is 50% off the original ticketed price. Once a year, usually in September, this venerable retailer holds a great ware-

---

women's fashion

house sale. You really can't beat that for quality Eddie Bauer clothing.
  201 Aviva Park Drive (first lights north of Steeles Ave. off Weston Road),
  Vaughan.
  Tel: 905-850-7016
  Hours: M. to F. 10 - 7, Sat. 10 - 6, Sun. 12 - 5

EMMANUEL BITINI FASHION OUTLET
  49 Orfus Rd., (west off Dufferin St., south of Hwy. 401), Toronto.
  Tel: 416-782-3211
  Hours: M. to Sat. 10-6, Sun. 12-5:30.

FEMINE LA FLARE INC. - IMPORTER'S OUTLET
  6130 Tomken Rd., (west side, between Derry Rd. and Hwy. 401),
  Mississauga.
  Tel: 905-564-1042
  Hours: M. to F. 9 - 5.

Can vegetarians eat animal crackers?

FREDA'S

We dropped in to see Freda this week and buy something special for the holidays. As always, she has a wonderful selection of marvellous clothes for women that include suits, sweaters and holidaywear. Right now she has her fall/winter sale on with savings of 25-50%, and up to 70% in her clearance section at the back.

86 Bathurst Street (one block south of King Street), Toronto.
Tel: 416-703-0304.
Website: www.fredas.com
Hours: M.-W. and Fri. 9- 6:00; Thu. 9-8; Sat. 9:30-6; Call for special Christmas hours.

GRANNY TAUGHT US HOW

This wonderful country store carries ladies clothing – Woolrich, Royal Robbins, Susan Bristol, Sigrid Olsen, Catherine Steward, Bellepointe and Eric Alexandre. Beautiful 100% cotton fabric and quilting, home décor items, Christmas items and other country apparel. Great sales in July and the end of November.

RR#4 Shelburne – (west on Hwy 89, and the store is between Airport Road and Hwy. 10), Shelburne.
Tel: 519-925-2748
Hours: M. to Thur., 10-6, Fri. to Sat. 10-9, Sun. 10-6

HOLT RENFREW LAST CALL

Don't miss this opportunity to pick up some real bargains on this season's winter merchandise now being cleared through this outlet store. Look for Holt's own label, as well as names like DKNY and Anne Klein. Ladies sportswear is on sale this week, and accessories and Brown's shoes go on sale March 13. Menswear starts March 20.

370 Steeles Ave. W. (between Yonge St. and Bathurst St.), Toronto
Tel: 905-886-7444
Hours: Store is open year round, but for Ladies Sportswear and Accessories, Brown's Shoes and Menswear, specific sales and times are help, usually in March, please call.

Corduroy pillows are making headlines.

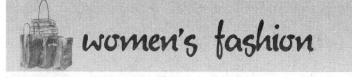
women's fashion

IMAGES THAT SUIT 🛍
At this year's semi-annual clearance sale, pricing is unbeatable on labels like Anne Klein, Doraz, JAX, Louden and many more. Their $20.00 rack is phenomenal! From suits, jackets, skirts and dress pants to T-shirts, sweaters and blouses, pick up unbeatable bargains at 50% to 80% off. Free parking and wheelchair accessible.

    6511A Mississauga Rd., (just below the 401 and Erin Mills Pkwy.) Mississauga, Tel: 905-814-7933.

    Hours: Call for 2002-3 sale dates and times.
See advertisement on page A12

LINEA INTIMA 🛍
A hot summer semi-annual sale from 30-70% off selected name brand sleepwear and robes. Specializing in imported bras and fittings. Enjoy savings on Lejaby, Chantelle, Dim, Simone Perele and more lovely intimate items.

    1925 Avenue Road (south of Hwy. #401) Toronto.

    Tel: 416-780-1726

    250 Wincott Drive. (Between Eglinton, and Islington.) Toronto

    Tel: 416-245-3633

    Hours: Mon. to Thur. 10 a.m. to 6 p.m. Friday and Saturday 10 a.m. to 5 p.m.

    Annual sales: Jan.-15-30 and July 15-30

JACK AND PETER'S PLACE
Peter tells us that they are in the midst of "cleaning house", and clearing out most of their spring and summer clothing. Lots of women's wear, and even some men's ties at discount prices.

If your summer stroll takes you to Spadina Avenue, be sure to drop in.

    161 Spadina Ave., Toronto.

    Tel: 416-971-5207

    Hours: Mon. - Sat. 8:30 - 5:30.

    Call for special sale events.

JAYSET - MANUFACTURER'S CLEARANCE STORES
    499 Main St., Shoppers World (NW corner of Steeles Ave. and Hwy. 10), Brampton.

    Tel: 905-450-5465

    Hours: M. to F. 10 - 9, Sat. 9:30 - 6, Sun. 12 – 5

    Call for other locations and hours.

JONES FACTORY FINALE

388 Applewood Cres. (west off Jane St., just south of Langstaff Rd.),
Vaughan.
Tel: 905-760-6068
Hours: M. to S. 9:30-6 and Sun. 12-5.
Call for other locations and hours.

LA CACHE OUTLET SALE 🏠

Enjoy a little trip to this fabulous outlet tucked into one of Hamilton's malls.
For everyone who loves designer April Cornell's bright colours and bold
designs you will find her dresses and linens at 75% off and more. This once a
year sale has tablecloths, napkins, duvet covers, bed linens, cushion covers, decorative tablewear and much more. At these prices, pick up a couple for gifts.

Jackson Square Mall, 2 King St. W., Hamilton, (Hwy. #401 west to Hwy.
#403, exit off York to Copps Coliseum, the mall is attached to Copps).
Tel: 905-528-3270
Call for sale dates and hours. M. to Sat. 10 - 5; Sun. 12 - 5

LANCE LORENTS LIMITED 🏠

Beautiful Italian sweaters and French tops, including twin sets and cardigans, in
cashmere and wool blends, merinos and merino blends, all available directly at
the importer's price. From their Emilio Bravini Collection you will find elegant
suits, separates and superb coats.

500 Glencairn Ave. Unit 2 (northwest corner of Bathurst St. and
Glencairn Ave, north of Eglinton Ave., south of Lawrence Ave.) Toronto.
Tel: 416-782-7864
Hours: Call for dates and time of sale. See advertisement on page A16

LEN'S MILL STORE

Len's has one of the largest ranges of home decorating fabrics we've seen. This
includes upholstery and quilting fabrics, as well as drapery hardware and
notions at very competitive prices. As well, you'll discover a huge assortment
of hand knitting yarns. And if you need hosiery for the family, check out their

---

Is a book on voyeurism a peeping tome?

---

brand name hosiery at bargain prices. Many locations in southwestern Ontario, with a superstore in Guelph.

  Eight locations in Ontario.
  Tel: Toll free: 1-888-536-7645 for a complete list,
  Website: www.lensmill.com.
  Hours: M.,T.,W. and Sat. 10- 5; Thu. and Fri. 10- 9; Sun. 12-5

L'ELEGANTE

For more than 30 years, providing the highest quality of upscale resale ladies fashions such as Chanel, Prada, Gucci, and Hermes.

  122 Yorkville Ave., Toronto
  Hours: M. T. W. & Fri. 10-6; Thu. 10-7; Sat. 10-6; Sun. 11-5.
  Tel: 416-923-3220
  Sherwood Forest Village, 1900 Dundas St. W., Mississauga.
  Hours: M. T. W. 10-6; Thu. Fri. 10-7; Sat. 9:30-5; Sun. closed
  Tel: 905-822-9610

See advertisement on page 171

LE CHATEAU - FASHION OUTLET

  47 Orfus Rd., Toronto.
  Tel: 416-787-4214
  Hours: M. to W. 10 - 6, Thu. & F. 10 - 9, Sat. 9:30 - 6, Sun. 12 - 6

LE FIRME

Everything must go at this "Closing Down for Italy" sale. Fabulous bargains of men and women's fashions on name brands such as Versace, Dolce, Ferre, Gucci, Prada Leather, Fendi and many more. You have to visit the showroom to believe some of their bargains. Alterations are extra and sales are final.

  95 East Beaver Creek Rd., Unit 3, (north of Hwy. #7, just east of
  Leslie St.) Richmond Hill.
  Tel: 905 -707-8727
  Hours: M-Sat. 11-6.

Dancing cheek-to-cheek is really a form of floor play.

---

women's fashion

LEVY'S DISCOUNT DESIGNER ORIGINALS - LADIES, MEN'S & CHILDRENS FASHIONS

Smart consumers regularly shop here for first quality, in-season designer outfits with at least 40 to 50% off retail prices.

541 St. Clair Ave. W., Toronto.

Tel: 416-653-9999

Hours: M. & T. 10 - 6:30, W., Thu. & F. 10 - 8, Sat. 10 - 6, Sun. 12 - 5

LIZ CLAIBORNE SAMPLE SALE/DKNY JEANS 🛍

If you're lucky enough to be a size 6 or 8, you'll love this sample sale. Spring and summer 2002 merchandise will be offered at great prices, including jackets starting at $25, blouses and shirts starting at $15 and much more. DKNY jeans will also be available in a range of sizes, and lots of accessories that include handbags, hats and belts. Savings of 30% or more everyday of fashions by Liz Claiborne Collection, Liz Claiborne for Women, Lizwear, Lizsport, Emma James. Villager Claiborne for Men and Accessories by Liz Claiborne.

6185 McLaughlin road (north of Britannia Road, west of Hurontario St.), Mississauga

Tel: 905-712-4130

Hours: Call for sale dates and hours.

See advertisement on page A13

LIZZY-B UNIFORM SALES

Stock up on various uniforms, especially those worn in the health services industry. Over 25 colours to choose from. All regular inventory is heavily discounted to clear.

85 Limestone Cres, North York.

Tel: 416-739-6662 or Toll Free: 1-800-268-8668

Hours: M. to F. 9 - 5

Sea captains don't like crew cuts.

LORNE'S FASHIONS - FACTORY OUTLET
Lorne designs coats and suits for some of North America's finest labels and you can find them here - minus labels for half the regular prices at his factory on Spadina. Ladies suits, jackets and slacks from $99. Alterations available.

101 Spadina Ave. (Between Queen St. & King St.), Toronto.
Tel: 416-596-1058
Hours: M. to Sat. 9 - 6, Sun. 10 - 6

LYNN FACTORY OUTLET
This outlet is open year round and stocks in-season brand name ladies clothes at deep discount prices. Sizes 4-20 from very casual to formal. Summer and winter deep discount sales.

116 Orfus Rd., North York.
Tel: 416-784-3052
Hours: M. - Thu. 10 - 6, F. 10 - 9, Sat. 9:30 - 6, Sun. 12 – 5

MAPLE HOSIERY SOCKS FACTORY OUTLET
This is a fairly new outlet with incredible deals on ladies and men's basic and fancy socks. We found extremely low priced soft-combed high quality cotton socks and seconds or slightly irregulars starting at only $1.00 a pair. Lots of fun patterns for teenagers and children. Good value here for the whole family!

26 Pine St. (first light west of Jane St., first building south of Lawrence) Toronto. Tel: 416 748-0369.
Hours: Monday to Friday 10 a.m. to 6 p.m., Saturdays 11 a.m. to 4 p.m.

Pokemon (n), A Jamaican proctologist

---

women's fashion

MARILYN'S

Marilyn Wetston has been called the Wardrobe Doctor. For 25 years she has offered designer clothing at discounts from 20-80%. Sizes range from 4-24 in smartly casual to elegant evening wear and new stock arrives weekly.

She and her staff will help you co-ordinate a complete new wardrobe, or find items to co-ordinate with your existing wardrobe. (Feel free to bring items with you.) You'll find mainly Canadian designers, and quality clothing at excellent prices, including a Cash & Carry Bridal Outlet with ready-to-wear Wedding & Bridesmaid Dresses and Accessories. Marilyn's goal is to have all customers leave with a positive wardrobe statement, not just clothes.

NEW ADDRESS August 1, 2002:
Still in the heart of the Garment District
200 Spadina Ave. (north of Queen St.), Toronto.
Tel: 416-504-6777
Hours: M.-F. 10-6; Sat. 10-5.

Does the name Pavlov ring a bell?

---

women's fashion

MARIKA's

Ladies high-end, quality European imports and name brands such as Frank Usher and Eugene Klein 705-, sportswear and accessories are clearing at up to 80% off. Lots of stock to choose from and the staff is extremely helpful. In house alterations are done for your convenience.

250 Wincott Drive, (north off Eglinton Ave., just west of Islington Ave. in the Richview Square Mall), Toronto.
Tel: 416-248-0999
Hours: Mon. to Wed. and Sat. 10 a.m. to 6 p.m., Thu. and Fri. 10 a.m to 7 p.m.

NORAMA DESIGN WAREHOUSE SALE

Great Bargains on a wide assortment of fleece, jackets, mock turtles, t-shirts and lots more at prices of 50 to 70% off. All sportswear items are either discontinued or excess inventories – no seconds.

475 Fenmar Drive (north of Finch Ave., and Weston Rd.) North York.
Tel: 416-744-6994
Call for sale dates and hours.

NORMA PETERSON FASHIONS

This Canadian designer and manufacturer of comfortable, casually elegant, machine washable fashions that are suitable for "a long day at the office" ,"an informal evening out" or "casual weekendwear". This Fall, along with the interlock knits and stretch suedes, they are introducing colourful boucles and cozy microfleece separates. Semi-annual sales include 40% discount and in some cases up to 80% off retail prices! Shelves are restocked daily.

women's fashion

Warehouse sales in Feb. and Aug.
> 82 Doncaster Avenue, Thornhill (north of Steeles, east from Yonge
> Street).
> Tel: 905-882-8221
> Hours: M.-W. 10-6; Thu., F. 10-7; Sat. 10 - 6; Sun. noon to 5.

PARKHURST - WAREHOUSE SALE 📦

Always a great sale at Parkhurst sweater outlet sale and your savings are up to
70% OFF. You will find lots of sweaters, gift sets, accessories and home accents
here. Shop early if you are looking for quality and stylish knitwear.
> 22 Research Road, Toronto (West of Leslie St., 2 blocks south of Eglinton
> Ave. East, off Brentcliffe Rd.) Park and enter south/east end of building.
> Tel: 416-421-3773
> Hours & Dates: Outlet sale every year in April, August, & November. Call
> for sale dates and times.

See advertisement on page A31

PEPPERTREE KLASSICS 📦

You'll find many of your favourite names that include Parkhurst sweaters,
French Dressing denim, Scotts washable suede, Kolosh, Jasmin and Amato
shoes and boots, plus lots more at this terrific store. When we were there, we
bought a pair of shoes as well as several accessories, from their wide selection. Prices are good year round, but are particularly slashed during their
Boxing Day event on December 26 when everything is 50% off.
> 137 Main Street N. (north of Hwy 7 on Hwy 48), Markham.
> Tel: 905-294-3882
> Hours: M.- S. 10 - 5:30
> Website: www.peppertree.ca

A successful diet is the triumph of mind over platter.

---

women's fashion

PHANTOM WAREHOUSE SALE - CLEARANCE OUTLET 🛍

This well-known manufacturer of hosiery and bodywear opened a 7,000 sq. ft. outlet of all their swimwear, bodywear, pantyhose, tights, aerobicwear, sportswear, panties, plus assorted socks at huge discounts. A real find and a great place to stock up on the basics. Don't miss also their semi-annual sale of hosiery, socks, tights, Gilda Marx bodywear, swimwear and accessories and their seamless apparel.

207 Weston Rd., Toronto.
Tel: 416 762-7177.
NEW LOCATION: Heartland Town Centre, 6045 Mavis Rd., Mississauga (Mavis Drive & Britannia)
Tel: 905 568-2258
Hours: Clearance centre – Monday to Friday 9:30 a.m. to 9 p.m., Saturday 9:30 a.m. to 6 p.m., Sunday 11 a.m. to 7 p.m.
Warehouse Sale held twice yearly, early November and late April.
Call 416-762-7177 for dates and times.

See advertisement on page A24

PICADILLY FASHIONS - LADIESWEAR FACTORY OUTLET

2825 Dufferin St. (east side, south of Lawrence Ave.), Toronto.
Tel: 416-783-1889
Hours: M. to F. 10:30 - 5, Sat. 10 - 3

PLEASANT PHEASANT SALE 🛍

Ruth Fox – award winning designer has lots of jackets and vests and tons of gloves for every occasion. They also have wonderful hats and caps. December Warehouse Sale.

35 Lisgar St. (at Queen St. and Dovercourt Ave.) Toronto.
Tel: 416-599-5408.
Hours: Monday to Friday 10 a.m. to 6 p.m., Saturday 10 a.m. to 4 p.m.

PORTOLANO GLOVE OUTLET

840 Walker Street (Edward St. South exit off the 401, west on Wood St., north on Walker St.), Prescott
Tel: 613-925-4242
Hours: Mon. to Sat. 10 a.m. to 4:30 p.m.

---

women's fashion

RAN'S MATERNITY WAREHOUSE SALE 📇

Drop in to their sales which feature seasonal merchandise ranging from 30 - 70% off. November Warehouse Sale.

20 Maud St., Suite 401 (west of Spadina Ave., between Richmond and Adelaide Sts.), Toronto.
Tel: 416-703-1744
Hours: Call for sale dates and hours.

RITCHÉ ANNUAL BRIDAL SALE 📇

The annual bridal sale that Canada's brides wait for. Choose from over 1000 designer wedding gowns greatly reduced! The sale also includes great deals on bridal accessories, headpieces and veils. There is also a fantastic selection of 705-, suits, mother of the bride and flower girl dresses. Four days only, don't miss it!

Tel: 416-789-4378
Hours: Call for 2003 dates and location
Website: www.ritchebridal.com

ROCOCO DESIGNERS OUTLET

14799 Yonge Street, Aurora.
Tel: 905-726-8977
Hours: - M. to Fri. 10-6, Thur. 10-9, Sat. 10-5.

ROMANTIC NIGHT BY LILIANNE - FACTORY OUTLET

4544 Dufferin St., Unit 13 (just south of Finch Ave.), Downsview.
Tel: 416-665-6181
Hours: M. to F. 9 - 5 with special hours for Christmas and Valentine's day.

SANDY WHITE

Sandy White has five stores in Toronto, as well as a location in Niagara-on-the-Lake. In their "bargain" room, located at the back of their main store, you'll find 30 to 70% off inventory that has been gathered from all their stores. Items will be either off season or surplus, and will include well known names like Sigrid Olsen, Jones of New York and many more. Well worth a visit.

3229 Yonge Street (3 blocks north of Avenue Road), Toronto
Tel: 416-482-6337
Hours: Monday to Friday 10:00 a.m. to 6:00 p.m., Saturday 9:30 a.m. to 5:30 p.m.

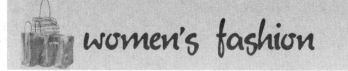

women's fashion

**You are reading the NEW 2003 Shoestring Shopping Guide
Your assurance of quality and value shopping.**

"Don't leave home without it"

PS: Shoestring makes a great "Stocking Stuffer" gift
with timely information about really great after Christmas sales.

SUNNY CHOI OUTLET STORE

Many of you may be familiar with this Canadian designer's line of clothing. At
this outlet store, you'll find suits, leisure wear, and a wonderful variety of
eveningwear Inventory is mainly out of season and last year's lines, but the
prices are 50 to 60% off regular prices.

370 Steeles Ave. W., Unit 106 (one block west of Yonge Street), Thornhill
Tel: 905-709-1678
Hours: Monday to Friday 10 a.m. to 9 p.m., Saturday 10 a.m. to 6 p.m.,
Sunday noon to 5 p.m.

SUPER SELLERS LINGERIE & ACTIVEWEAR

First quality brand name lingerie, fitness wear and a large selection of thongs,
pantyhose, stay-ups, stockings and fishnet products discounted everyday 25-
50%. Brand names include; DIM, WARNERS, PAPILLON BLANC, SKINNY,
ELITA, TRIUMPH, GILDAMARX, MONDOR, SPEEDO AND MUCH MORE.
Our expert staff will stay with you until the fit is just right.

488 Yonge St. (1-1/2 blocks north of College St.), Toronto.
Tel: 416-925-5031
Hours: M. to F. 10 - 7:30, Sat. 10 - 6:30, Sun. 1-5.

TALBOTS OUTLET

Looking for a real deal? At Talbot's outlet store you will discover 25% to 70%
discounts off every day on past season clothing from their misses, petites and
accessories and shoe collections. New selections arrive on a regular basis.

16 Famous Avenue, Unit 146 , Colossus Centre at Weston Road and
Highway #7, Woodbridge.
Tel: 905-660-0500
Hours: Mon. to Fri.10 a.m. to 9 p.m, Sat. 9:30 a.m. to 6 p.m.,
Sun. 11 a.m. to 5

women's fashion

THE LINGERIE HOUSE
2098 Queen St. E. (Beaches), Toronto.
Tel: 416-699-1804
Hours: Call for store hours

THINK TWICE
March Break is around the corner.....and you're headed south with nothing to wear!! Drop into Think Twice where they have recently received a large shipment of new spring and summer wear. Favourite labels include Louben, Jones New York, Studio Jax, and many more. Of course winter merchandise is also being cleared. We've found some terrific items in this store, and service is very friendly.

1679 Lakeshore Road W. (4 km. West of Mississauga Rd.), Mississauga.
Tel: 905-823-2233
Hours: Monday to Friday 10 a.m. to 5:30 p.m., Saturday 10 a.m. to 5 p.m.
See advertisement on page A20

TOM'S PLACE WAREHOUSE SALE 💲
Lots of famous-name designer clothes will be featured at 60-80% off retail. Look for business attire for both men and women, with Tom's expert retail staff on hand to help with fittings. A portion of proceeds will be donated to the Bloor JCC.

Bloor Jewish Community Centre. 750 Spadina Avenue (close to the Spadina subway) Toronto.
Tel: 416-924-6211.
Hours: October 26-29. Thursday and Friday 11:00 a.m. - 8:00 p.m., Saturday and Sunday 10:00 a.m. - 6:00 p.m.
See advertisement on page A9

TONI PLUS WAREHOUSE OUTLET 💲
A unique fashion outlet that caters to sophisticated plus size customers in sizes 14-22. Lots of name brand labels at this outlet including Jones New York, Ellen Tracy, Ralph Lauren and more. New arrivals just in are up to 50% off and final reductions on last season's stock up to 90% off with lots of selection..

1140 Sheppard Ave. West, Unit 16, Downsview (just west of the Allen Expressway) Toronto.
Tel: 416-633-9331 ext. 34
Hours: Open 7 days/week. M.-Sat. 10-6; Sun. noon to 5.
See advertisement on page A24

 women's fashion

WARDEN POWER CENTRE DESIGNER SAMPLE SALE 💲
The designers are ready, the racks are full and the buys are a steal. If you have the opportunity to drop into this one day sale, you'll be delighted with brand names that include David Dixon Designs, Zrihen and Chun Inc., Jules Power and more. Choose from a full range of women's contemporary clothing . Cash only, all sales final.

Warden Power Centre (just north of St. Clair Ave.), Toronto.
Tel: 416-752-4212
Hours: Call for date and time of 2002-3 sale.

WARNER'S - FACTORY OUTLET STORE
Dixie Outlet Mall, 1250 South Service Rd., (off the QEW between Dixie and Cawthra Rds.) Mississauga.
Tel: 416-285-4389
Hours: Call For location and sale dates M. to F. 10 – 9,
Sat. 9:30 - 6, Sun. 12 - 5

WINNERS
60 locations across Ontario.
Toll free: 1-877-WINN-877
Call for hours and location nearest you

Two banks with different rates have a conflict of interest.

Reading whilst sunbathing makes you well-red.

---

women's fashion

ZACKS – FASHION OUTLET 🛍

The latest Women's fashions with everyday savings up to 70% including twice a year end of season clearance of all regular Zack's merchandise as seen in malls across Southern Ontario and the G.T.A. Five locations to serve you.

Toronto - 2501 Steeles Ave. West Toronto.
Tel: 416-736-1638
Guelph – Willow West Mall
135 Silvercreek Parkway
Tel: 519-824-0420
Cambridge – 63 Main St.
Tel: 519-621-4206
Tillsonburg – Tillsonburg
Towne Centre,
200 Broadway St.
Tel: 519- 842-7482
Waterloo - 31 King St. North.
Tel: 519- 886-4980
Hours: Call for Hours

since 1921
FASHION OUTLET

Every day savings up to 70% off including twice a year end of season clearance of all reular Zacks merchandise as seen in major malls across Southern Ontario and the G.T.A.

Five Locations to serve you!!

GUELPH:
Willow West Mall
135 Silvercreek
Parkway
(519) 824-0420

TILLSONBURG:
Tillsonburg Town
Centre
200 Broadway St.
(519) 842-7482

WATERLOO:
31 King St. N.
(519) 886-4980

TORONTO:
2501 Steeles Ave. W.
(416) 736-1638

CAMBRIDGE:
63 Main St.
(519) 621-4206

Hours vary by location. So please call.

Time flies like an arrow. Fruit flies like a banana.

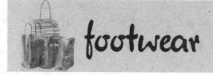
footwear

ALDO - CLEARANCE OUTLET

332 Yonge St. (northwest corner at Dundas St.), Toronto.
Tel: 416-596-1390
Hours: M. to F. 10 - 9, Sat. 10 - 6, Sun. 12 - 5
Call for other locations.

BATA SHOE OUTLET/ ATHLETES WORLD OUTLET

Dixie Outlet Mall, (Dixie Rd. and Q.E.W.), Mississauga.
Tel: 905-271-6814
Athletes World.
Tel: 905-271-9218
Hours: M. to F. 10 - 9, Sat. 9:30 - 6, Sun. 12-6

BOCCI SHOES - OUTLET STORE

When Bocci's regular retail outlets are down to their last three or four pairs
of shoes, they're sent to Bocci's warehouse. Chances of finding some current
styles are good. The footwear is organized by size and savings are up to 70%.
Bocci carries only men's and women's shoes - none for children.

1126 Finch Ave. W., Downsview.
Tel: 416-736-1732
Hours: M. to F. 10 - 6, Sat. 10 - 5, Sun. 12 - 5

BROOKS WAREHOUSE SALE 🏺

If you are looking for athletic footwear, apparel or casual shoes, drop in here.
Save up to 70% off retail on three-in-one coats with removable liners, fleece, T-
shirts for only $7.50, golf shirts and more. They carry names such as
Wolverine, Brooks, CAT, Avia, Guess, Caterpillar and more in this big semi-
annual sale.

520 Abilene Dr., (north of Hwy. #401, west of Hwy. #410, right off
Kennedy Rd.) Mississauga.
Tel: 905-564-6830.
Hours: Call for 2002-3 sale dates and hours.

CANLY SHOES

180 Steeles Ave. W., Thornhill.
Tel: 905-886-2363/4379
Hours: M. to F. 10 - 9, Sat. 10 - 6, Sun. 12 - 5
Call for other locations.

footwear

DACK'S SHOES
  595 Trethewey Dr. (S. of Lawrence Ave., E. of Jane St.), Toronto.
  Tel: 416-241-5216.
  Hours: M. to Sat. 9-6

FACTORY SHOE
In the shoe business since 1956, this outlet features better buys on a wide
assortment of footwear for the whole family, as well as quite a selection of
safety shoes and boots.
  1151 Upper James Street, (Upper James at Lincoln Alexander Parkway),
  Hamilton.
  Tel: 905-318-9799
  Hours: M. to F. 9 - 9, Sat. 9 - 6, Sun. 11 - 5

FOOTWEAR FACTORY OUTLET
  29 Plains Rd. W., Burlington.
  Tel: 905-681-3338
  Hours: M. to Thu. 10 - 6, F. 10 - 5, Sat. 10 - 6, Sun. 12 – 5
  Call for other location.

GERTEX FACTORY OUTLET
  9 Densley Ave. (E. off Keele St., 3 streets S. of Lawrence Ave.), Toronto.
  Tel: 416-241-2345
  Hours: M. to F. 8:30-5

GORDON CONTRACT
  552 Queen Street West (east of Bathurst Street), Toronto.
  Tel: 416-504-5503
  Hours: M. to F. 10 - 5, Sat. 10 – 4
  Call for other locations.

INGEBORG'S SHOES - WAREHOUSE OUTLET
  1681 Finfar Ct., Mississauga.
  Tel: 905-823-7415
  Hours: M. to Sat. 9 - 5, Sun. 11 - 4

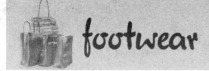
footwear

JOE SINGER SHOES LIMITED
53 Orfus Road, (west off Dufferin Street, south of Hwy 401), Toronto.
Tel: 416 - 782-1281
Hours: M., T., W. Sat. 10-6; Thu., Fri., 10-8 Sun. 11-4.

KANGAROOS SHOE WAREHOUSE SALE 🏺
180 West Beaver Creek Road (Hwy 7 and Leslie St.), Richmond Hill.
Tel: 905-889-7642
Hours: Call for 2002-3 sale dates and hours.

LITTLE SHOE PALACE
3189 Bathurst St. (S. of Hwy. 401), Toronto.
Tel: 416-785-5290
Hours: M. to W. & F. 10 - 6, Thu. 10 - 7:30, Sun. 10 - 5
(Closed Saturdays). Call for other location.

McGREGOR SOCKS FACTORY OUTLETS
These outlets offer brand name socks and hosiery at up to 50% off - and have
a pricing structure in place that lets you save more the more you buy. Brands
include Calvin Klein, Levi's, GUESS, Dockers and popular McGregor brands like
Weekender, Premium and Happyfoot. Great deals on irregular and disconting-
ued items. Bring some friends and take advantage of bulk discounts. "Their
prices will knock your socks off!"
30 Spadina Avenue, Toronto
Tel: 416-593-5353, ext. 344
Hours: M. to Sat. 10-5
70 The East Mall at the Queensway, Toronto.
Tel: 416-252-3716, ext. 450
Hours: Tue.-Sat. 10-5
1360 Birchmount Road (just north of Lawrence Ave.), Scarborough.
Tel: 416-751-5511, ext. 5511
Hours: Tue.-Fri. 10-6; Sat. 10-5

See advertisement on page A15

Condoms should be used on every conceivable occasion.

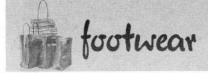
footwear

MAPLE HOSIERY SOCKS FACTORY OUTLET

This is a fairly new outlet with incredible deals on ladies and men's basic and fancy socks. We found extremely low priced soft combed high quality cotton socks, seconds or slightly irregulars starting at only $1.00 a pair. Lots of fun patterns for teenagers and children. Good value here for the whole family!

    26 Pine St. (first light west of Jane St., first building south of Lawrence) Toronto.
    Tel: 416-748-0369.
    Hours: M.-F. 10 a.m. to 6 p.m., Sat. 11 a.m. to 4 p.m.

MONDO MILANO SHOE WAREHOUSE

    39 Orfus Road (south of Hwy. 401, east off Dufferin Street), Toronto.
    Tel: 416-781-0414
    Hours: M.-W. + Sat. 10 - 6; Thu. and Fri. 10 - 9 Sun. 11 - 5.

THE NEXT STEP - CLEARANCE STORE

    Dixie Outlet Mall, 1250 South Service Rd., (southwest corner of Dixie Rd. and Q.E.W.), Mississauga.
    Tel: 905-891-3458.
    Hours: M. to F. 10 - 9, Sat. 9:30 - 6, Sun. noon - 6.

PAYLESS SHOESOURCE

    237 Yonge Street (just south of Dundas Street), Toronto.
    Tel: 416-362-6415
    Hours: M. to F. 10 - 9, Sat. 10 - 8, Sun. 12 – 6
    Call for other locations.

REEBOK - WAREHOUSE OUTLET

    201 Earl Stewart Dr. (north on Bayview Ave from Aurora Rd.), Aurora.
    Tel: 905-727-0704
    Call for other locations.

RHODES INC. - FACTORY OUTLET

    21 Steinway Blvd. #1, (1 block W. of Hwy. 27 off Steeles Ave.), Etobicoke.
    Tel: 416-674-8541

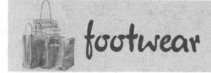 footwear

RUNNING FREE
Nick has scored some great buys from several suppliers including Nike, Adidas and Reebok. So look for great savings on sports apparel and footwear for the whole family.
709 Dennison St., Markham.
Tel: 905-477-7871 or for sale information call: 416-410-FREE
Hours: Call for hours.

SATIN 'N PARTY SHOES
With prom season in full bloom, you might want to check out this store that carries a large selection of satin and crepe shoes in all sizes. Purses also available. Custom dyeing takes about a week, and is available in all colours. Prices start at $34.99.
184 Spadina Ave. (north of Queen St.), Toronto.
Tel: 416-504-8823
Hours: M.-F.-11:30-5:30. Sat. 11-5

THE SHOE CLUB
There's no membership fee here, only tremendous savings on imported shoes and bags from Spain for the entire family. Call to find a location nearest you.
Tel: 905-820-3668

A gossip is someone with a great sense of rumor.

She criticized my apartment, so I knocked her flat.

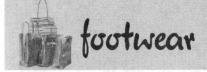 footwear

THE SHOE COMPANY

The buying power of 40+ superstores means they can offer you up to 50% off brand name fashion footwear everyday. They offer well defined women's, men's and kids departments in a no pressure environment. Shop on your own, or ask one of their well-trained service staff for assistance. Call 1-8888SHOECO for hours and a location near you.

Brampton
Trinity Common Hwy 410 N & Bovaird Rd.
905 - 789-8181

Markham
Woodside Mall
905 - 477-2224
Heartland Centre
Churchill Dr.
905 - 712-4949
Hwy 401 & Winston Churchill Dr.
905 - 824-9774
Oakville, Oakville Town Centre II
905 - 338-8285

Toronto
Lawrence Plaza
416 -787-5136

Yonge St. & Bloor St.
416 -923-8388
Yonge St. & Eglinton Ave.
416 -481-8448

Cambridge
Bridgecam Shopping
Centre
519- 622-6647
Mississauga
Dixie Value Mall
905 - 274-3861
Dundas St. W & Winston
905) 608-0266

Markham, Riocan Centre
905 - 895-9161
Scarborough, Warden Ave
& Eglinton.Ave
416 -751-1441
Bank Of Nova Scotia
King St. & Bay St.
(Concourse Level)
416 -360-7480
Yonge St. & Dundas
416 -594-1222
Colossus Centre
905 - 850-8081

See advertisement on page A14

**When you dream in color,
it's a pigment of your imagination.**

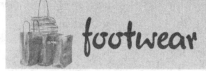 footwear

CLEARANCE OUTLET

44 Kodiak Cr. Last season's merchandise always 50% off or more.
Other locations in: Ajax, Ancaster, Barrie, Burlington, Gloucester, Kanata, Kingston,
Kitchener, London, Nepean, Ottawa, Sudbury, Alberta, British Columbia, Manitoba, New Brunswick and Nova Scotia.

SHOE HEAVEN WAREHOUSE OUTLET

51 Hurontario St., Collingwood.
Tel: 705-444-2863
Hours: M. to Thur. 9 - 6, Fri. 9 - 9 Sat. 9 - 6, Sun. 12 - 4

SHOE MACHINE - FACTORY OUTLET

130 Orfus Rd., 2nd floor (at Caledonia Rd.), Toronto.
Tel: 416-787-1451
Hours: M. to Sun. 7:30 - 4

TOOTSIES FAMILY SHOE MARKET

298 Wayne Gretzky Parkway, Unit 6, Brantford.
Tel: 519-754-4775
Call for other locations.

VARESE SHOES - OUTLET CENTRE

This Company has been in business for over 42 years and this outlet stocks mostly Italian imported men's and ladies shoes, including Timberland shoes and clothing apparel. They offer up to 70% off retail prices on seasonal and off-season merchandise.

51 Orfus Rd., North York.
Tel: 416-784-1330
Hours: M. to W. 10 - 6, Thu. & F. 9:30 - 9, Sat. 10 - 6, Sun. 11 – 6

> **Without geometry, life is pointless.**

bridal fashions and accessories

BEA SHAWN BRIDAL FASHIONS 🏺
389 Main St. N., Brampton.
Tel: 905-457-3363
Hours: M. to W. 10 - 6, Thu. & F. 10 - 9, Sat. 9:30 - 6

ELIZABETH STUART DISCOUNT BRIDAL
1015 Matheson Blvd., Unit 9 (south-east corner of Tomken Rd. and Matheson Blvd.), Mississauga.
Tel: 905-238-6856
Hours: T., W. & F. 11 - 6, Thu. 11 - 8, Sat. 10 - 3

FLOWERS & GIFTS BY WANDA
5 Waterbeach Cres., Etobicoke.
Tel: 416-742-7433
Hours: Please call for appointment.

LADY ANGELA GIFTS AND BOMBONIERE
This distributor of bombonieres, or wedding favours, carries hundreds of spools of ribbon, doilies and favours. If you like, the store can assemble and accessorize everything for you. It carries thank you gifts for showers, ushers and bridesmaids.
260 Geary Ave. Toronto.
Tel: 416 –533-4438
Hours: M. to W. 9 - 6, T. & F. 9-8, Sat. 9 - 6

SATIN PARTY SHOES
This great little store carries a wide range of styles in satin and crepe wedding shoes and purses. Custom shoe dyeing to match your outfit is available.
184 Spadina Ave., (north of Queen St.), Toronto.
Tel: 416-504-8823
Hours: M. to F. 12-5:30; Sat. 11:30-5:30

Arbitrator - A cook who leaves Arby's to work at Mc Donald's

---

bridal fashions and accessories

TUXEDO ROYALE 🛍

New wool blend tuxedos start at $199.00 and previously enjoyed ones at $99. All new accessories are a minimum 20% off, with a few slashed by as much as 70%. October Warehouse Sale.

185 Konrad Cres. (south of Hwy. 7 between Hwy. 404 & Woodbine Ave.), Markham.
Tel: 416-798-7617;
Web site: www.tuxedoroyale.com
Hours: Call for date and time of sale.

VALERIE SMYTH BRIDAL FASHIONS

Pickering.
Tel: 905-839-5335
Hours: By appointment only. Please call.

VILLAGE WEDDING BELLES

331 Dundas St. E. (east of Hwy. 6 on Hwy. 5), Waterdown.
Tel: 905-689-3150
Hours: M. to. F. 10 - 5:30, Thu. 10 - 8:30, Sat. 9:30 - 4:30, Sun. 1 - 4 (seasonal from January to June).

Primate - Removing your spouse from in front of the TV.

Polarize - What penguins see with.

ACCESSORY CONCEPTS INC. 🔖

Savings up to 75% off a large selection of Wallets, Back Packs, Luggage, Travel Acessories, Hand Bags, Sportswear, Leather Jackets and Winter Accessories. They also have a large selection of Coismetic Accessories and Gift Sets, featuring such names as Samsonite, Oscar Dela Renta, Fina, Heys, Everlite and Sambro.

> 5900 Keaton Cres., (corner Matheson, west of Hwy. #10), Mississauga.
> Tel: 905-712-8343
> Hours: Call for sale dates and hours.

ARTISTIC JEWELLERY

> 5511 Steeles Ave. W., unit 6 (east of Weston Rd.), North York.
> Tel: 416-742-6008 or Toll Free: 1-877-810-1304
> Hours: M.-F. 9-5.

A. J. COLONIAL DESIGNS 🔖

This manufacturer of designer jewellery has a year end liquidation of current fashion samples and factory overruns at 60-80% savings. Pick up brooches that retail from $7.99 to $18.99 each at $3.00 or a necklace that retails from $12.99 to $24.99 each at $5.00 each or earrings at $3.00 pair. Price includes PST & GST. A great, two weekend sale for special ladies.

> 70 Production Drive, Scarborough (south of 401 on Markham Rd., first intersection is Progress, turn right, first street left is Production).
> Tel: 416-289-0911
> Hours: Fri. Dec. 6th. and Fri. Dec. 13th 12noon-7pm.
> Sat. Dec. 7th. and Sat. Dec. 14th. 9am to 4pm.

jewellery and accessories

FASHION ACCESSORIES - WAREHOUSE OUTLET 🏷

It's small but packed with deals on hosiery, ladies socks and leggings, belts, slippers and some aerobic wear. There will be a big November warehouse sale. Cash and cheques with I.D. only. November and July Warehouse Sale.

34 Wingold Avenue (west off Dufferin St., south of Lawrence Ave.), Toronto.

Tel: 416-792-9500

Hours: Call for dates and times.

GARBO GROUP 🏷

As everyone knows, it's accessories that make the outfit, so make a quick trip to this sale to pick up some new jewellery or perhaps a scarf. You'll recognize many of the name brands such as Napier and Nine West. Accessories such as hair clips, head bands and glittery pins to complete your party outfit, make this sale a must. Cash only.

34 Wingold Avenue (north of Eglinton Avenue, west off Dufferin Street), Toronto.

Tel: 416-782-9500 or e-mail: garbo@garbo.ca.

Call for sale dates and times.

K-JAMSON LUGGAGE WAREHOUSE

Here you will find thousands of luggage, briefcases, handbags, school bags, evening purses, wallets, and holiday gifts up to 70% off regular prices. Name brands at this sale include Samsonite, Atlantic, American Tourister, Samboro and more. If you are looking for gifts for some youngsters, check out the neat children's travel and school bags at greatly reduced prices.

42 Riviera Drive (east of Woodbine Ave., north of Steeles Ave.), Markham.

Tel: 905-475-1282.

Hours: Call for sale dates. Monday to Friday 10a.m. to 7 p.m., Saturday 10 a.m. to 6 p.m., and Sunday 11 a.m. to 5 p.m.

JES HANDBAG DESIGN

53 Orfus Road Toronto (west off Dufferin Street, south of Hwy #401), Toronto.

Tel: 416 - 784-5266

Hours: M. T. W. Sat. 10-6;. Th.. F. 10-8; Sun. 11-4.

jewellery and accessories

MODERN WATCH CANADA

Newly renovated, a unique 3,000 sq. ft. showroom offering high quality Seiko, Citizen, Omega, Longines, Breitling, Gucci, Tag Heuer and many more watches. If you have a watch in mind for a special gift, check with them before you buy. They have wholesale prices and are open to the public. You can also visit their website at www.watchwholesale.com.

835 Kipling Avenue (south of Dundas), Toronto.
Hours: M.-F. 10-7; Sat. 10-6; Closed Sunday

See advertisement on page A16

PLEASANT PHEASANT 🏠

Ruth Fox – award winning designer has lots of jackets and vests and tons of gloves for every occasion. They also have wonderful hats and caps. December Warehouse Sale.

401 Richmond St. W., Suite 124, Toronto.
Tel: 416-599-5408
Hours: M. to F. 8 - 6

PORTOLANO GLOVE OUTLET

840 Walker Street (Edward St. South exit off the 401, west on Wood St., north on Walker St.), Prescott.
Tel: 613-925-4242
Hours: M.- Sat. 10-4:30.

Why don't sheep shrink when it rains?

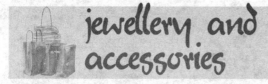

jewellery and accessories

SUNGLASS SAFARI

As always, when the spring sun starts to shine, most of us think about a new pair of sunglasses – or "sunnies" as my sister in Australia says! With over 2,000 brand name sunglasses and accessories on display, you're bound to find something at this sale. Everything is priced at 25 – 75% off regular price and comes with a one-year warranty.

2601 Matheson Blvd. East, Unit 3 (north of Centennial Park), Mississauga
Tel: 905-629-8333
Hours: Call for sale dates and hours.

jewellery and accessories

TILLEY WAREHOUSE SALE 🏺
Great gifts for everyone on your list at this outlet sale. We found golf accessories, scarves, hats, umbrellas, men's and women's wallets, handbags, gloves, luggage, briefcases, agendas, sports bags, backpacks and men's and women's leather coats at up to 70% off retail prices.

1314 Blundell Rd. (south of Dundas St., north of The Queensway, between Cawthra Rd. and Dixie Rd.) Mississauga.
Tel: 905 279-8844.
Hours: Call for exact sale dates and hours.

TIMEX - CLEARANCE OUTLET
445 Hood Rd. (W. of Warden Ave., N. off Denison St.), Markham.
Tel: 905-477-8463
Hours: M. to F. 8 - 4

VIVAH
Dixie Outlet Mall, 1250 South Service Road, Mississauga.
Tel: 905-278-8418
Hours: M. to F. 10 - 9, Sat 9:30 - 6, Sun. 12 - 6
Call for other location.

When two egotists meet, it's an I for an I.

---

sportwear and gear

ASH CITY WAREHOUSE SALE

We found some great deals at this sale – particularly if you have a golfer on your Christmas list. This company sells logowear to corporate clients, so are clearing out their shirts, jackets, outerwear and fleece products. We found a great jacket for $30, and golf shirts are 2/$15. This is the last weekend of the sale – VISA and cash only.

2071 McCowan Road (north of Sheppard Ave.), Scarborough
Tel: 416-292-6612
Hours: Call for sale dates and times.

BANFF DESIGNS FACTORY SALE

Once a year this sale is a terrific opportunity to pick up outerwear in Goretex, Protex and Polar Fleece at 50% off retail.. Clothing for everything from snowboarding and skiing to golfing and walking the dog. Lots of fleece accessories for gifts under $10.00..

53A Fraser Avenue (King Street and Dufferin Street), Toronto.
Tel: 416-588-4839
Hours: Sale date: November 30, 2002. Call for hours.

BIG CHIEF CANOE COMPANY

5781 Hwy. 7 (south side of 7, just east of Hwy. 27 behind Leisure Marine), Vaughan.
Tel: 905-856-4301
Hours: M to F. 7-6; Sat. 9-4; Closed Sunday.

BROOKS WAREHOUSE SALE

If you are looking for athletic footwear, apparel or casual shoes, drop in here. Save up to 70% off retail on three-in-one coats with removable liners, fleece, T-shirts for only $7.50, golf shirts and more. They carry names such as Wolverine, Brooks, CAT, Avia, Guess, Caterpillar and more in this big semi-annual sale.

520 Abilene Dr., (north of Hwy. #401, west of Hwy. #410, right off Kennedy Rd.), Mississauga.
Tel: 905-564-6830.
Hours: Call for sale dates and hours.

sportwear and gear

BROWN'S SPORTS
2447 Bloor St. W. (at Jane St.), Toronto.
Tel: 416-763-4176
Hours: M. to W. 9:30 - 6, Thu. & F. 9:30 - 8, Sat. 9:30 - 5:30

BRUZER SPORTS GEAR FACTORY SALE 🗑
For all you wakeboarders, skateboarders, snowboarders or even someone who likes to watch by the sidelines, come and check out this Canadian manufacturer's factory store. They specialize in really cool boarder gear for men and women. With huge sales 4 times a year, there is always a bargain to be found. Check out their web site www.bruzer.com for more information.
1203 Caledonia Rd., (brick building on the corner of Caledonia and Orfus Rds.)
Tel: 416-781-0011 x228
Hours: M to F. 10-7, Sat. 10-6, Sun. 12-5.
See advertisement on page A4

CANADA SPORTSWEAR
230 Barmac Drive (south of Steeles Ave., and west of Weston Road), North York.
Tel: 416-740-8020
Hours: M.-F. 10-6; Sat. 9-5.

CANADIAN SKI PATROL SKI SWAP 🗑
We are fortunate to have free ski patrolling in Canada - in some countries you have to negotiate a fee before being removed from the mountains after an injury! This huge ski swap is one way that they raise funds to continue their important work. It also presents an excellent way to pick up used equipment. There is a fee into the show but for enthusiasts, the Toronto Ski Show is a must. Ski show is mid-October.
Exhibition Place on Toronto's waterfront.
Tel: 416 -745-7511

COLLINGWOOD SKI CLUB SKI SWAP 🗑
It's always well done with excellent bargains and always takes place during the Thanksgiving weekend. You can sell and buy everything from new and used equipment to clothing. The sale is in October.
Central Base Lodge, Blue Mountain Resorts, seven miles west of Collingwood on Blue Mountain Rd. Collingwood.
Tel: 705-445-0231

sportwear and gear

CSA CANADA WAREHOUSE SALE

119 Franklin St. (take 401 to Bloomington Side Rd., go north to Uxbridge, turn right on Brock right on Franklin) Uxbridge.
Tel: 905-852-8826
Hours: M. to F. 9-4, Sat. 10-5

EUROPE BOUND

If you are into the great outdoors, don't miss these bargains. This semi-annual one-day sale on all their rental gear includes snowshoes, ice climbing gear, backpacks, tents and sleeping bags at half off regular retail prices. Get there early for best selection.

47 Front Street East (just west of Church Street on south side), Toronto.
Tel: 416-601-1990
Hours: Please call for annual September sale date and hours.

GEAR FOR SPORTS CANADA - WAREHOUSE SALE

380 Bentley St. (north of Steeles Ave. E. on Warden Ave. go west of Denison St. and north on Hood Rd. to Bentley), Markham.
Tel: 905-470-0404
Hours: T. to F. 11 - 6, Sat. 11 - 5

GEORGE BOND SPORTS WAREHOUSE SALE

This sale has become a real institution for those looking for ski and outer-wear. Samples, ends of lines and some seconds abound at this well stocked sale which includes jackets, snowsuits, ski accessories, fleece and much more. We saw children's insulated jackets for $9.99, and men's three-in-one jackets for $19.99. No cheques. All sales final.

2345 Matheson Blvd. East (West off Hwy. 427, north off Eglinton Ave., East of Orbitor Drive), Mississauga.
Hours: Mon – Fri. noon - 4pm
Tel: 905-602-4123 (Call for sale date(s).

See advertisement on page A26

GOLF TOWN

With a short golf vacation looming, we looked around for a store with a wide selection and competitive pricing – and found Golf Town, Canada's Golf Superstore. They have the guaranteed lowest prices on all the top brand names in golf equipment and supplies, including; clubs, bags, balls, shoes, apparel and accessories. In fact anything to do with golf can be found at Golf Town. We were even able to try out our clubs before we bought them. We tried out several different clubs in their golf simulators where you can play on any course in the world. Before we left we took advantage of their certified CPGA pros that give you a lesson right in the store. Now we know why they call it Golf Town, because they have everything to do with golf and more! You can also visit them on-line at www.golftown.com.

Markham: 3265 Highway 7 East (Woodbine & Hwy. 7)
Tel: 905 - 479-6978
Mississauga: 3050 Vega Blvd. (Dundas & Hwy. 403)
Tel: 905 - 569-2088
Scarborough: Kennedy Commons (Kennedy & Hwy. 401)
Tel: 416 -335-4888
Woodbridge: 55 Colossus Dr. (Hwy. 400 & Hwy. 7)
Tel: 905 - 264-8809

GREENHAWK HARNESS & EQUESTRIAN
SUPPLIES SALE WAREHOUSE

This is one of the largest sales of riding apparel and horse supplies in Canada. Their famous semi-annual sale is on for only three days with prices slashed from a minimum of 15% right up to 50%. You'll discover just about everything you could think of to do with horses, including saddles, harnesses, boots, bits and other horse equipment, as well as a full selection of riding apparel.

5700 Keaton Cres., Unit 1 (Between Hurontario St. and Mavis Rd., just off Matheson Blvd.), Mississauga.
Tel: 905-238-5502
Hours: April 24, 25, 26 and October 23, 24, 25. 10am to 6pm.

sportwear and gear

INLINE & ICE SKATE LIQUIDATION

No better time than now to buy that pair of inline skates you keep promising yourself you're going to try. This sale includes manufacturer's samples, over-runs and odd colours all of first quality and with full warranty. Trained staff will help you with sizing and requirements. Skates will be 30 - 60% off retail, and include OXYGEN OZ series skates Abec 3 (it's a skating term for the bearings in the wheels!), Abec 1 hockey boots with aluminum chassis and high end children's skates starting at $29.95. The majority of skates are priced between $75 and $150.........as well, there will be a selection of new and used hockey equipment at heavily discounted prices. Wheelchair accessible. Call for warehouse sale(s) details.

> North York Centennial Centre Arena, 580 Finch Ave. W. (Bathurst St. and Finch Ave. area, opposite Branson Hospital), North York.
> Tel: 416 -663-5841
> Hours: M. to F. 10- 8, Sat. & Sun. 10 - 5; please call for summer hours.

JOTANI SPORTSWEAR - CATALOGUE OUTLET SALE 🛍

Ladies golf fashion for on and off the course. Tee off with great savings - up to seventy per cent off retail - as this outlet clears out excess stock from their mail order company. Call for a free catalogue. Web Site: www.jotani.com

> 604 Edward Ave. Unit 3, (west of Bayview Ave., north off Elgin Mills), Richmond Hill.
> Tel: 1-800-431-9997
> Hours: Please call for hours and sale dates.

MR. BILLIARD

And now for something just a little different. If you're in the market for a pool table, slot machine or poker table, there's no better selection.

> 515 Britannia Rd. E., Mississauga.
> Tel: 905-696-0600; Toll free: 1-800-661-0106
> Web site; www.mrbilliard.com.
> Hours: M. to F. 9 - 5

NATIONAL SPORTS EQUIPMENT REPAIR

> 1540 Lodestar Rd., Unit 5 (west off Dufferin St./Allen Rd., north of Sheppard), Downsview.
> Tel: 416-638-3408
> Hours: M. to F. 8:30 - 5:30

sportwear and gear

NEWSON'S BIKE AND SKATE EXCHANGE
612 Jane St. (at Dundas St.), Toronto.
Tel: 416-762-9976
Hours: T. to Thu. 8:30 - 6, F. 8:30 - 8:30, Sat. 8:30 – 5

NORTH FACE OUTLET
Cookstown Manufacturers Outlet Mall, (south east corner of Hwy. 400
and Hwy. 89), Cookstown.
Tel: 705- 458-8400.
Hours: M. to F. 10-9, Sat. and Sun. 9-6

NORTH YORK CENTENNIAL PRO SHOP SALE
Big sale on for sports enthusiasts looking for inline skates and hockey equip-
ment for two days only. The inline skates and accessories will be priced at up
to 75% off with the majority of them under $100.00. This year's ice hockey
equipment up to 50% off all new brand names. Staff will be available to help
you with fitting. Ample parking available.
North York Centennial Arena, 580 Finch Ave, West (one block west of
Bathurst St.), North York.
Tel: 416-663-5841
Hours: Call for date and time.

OLD FIREHALL SPORTS 🏬
We dropped in to visit this week while in Unionville, and were impressed by
the value and selection in this sports store. With the mild weather this year,
they find themselves with lots of inventory to clear during their annual sale.
Everything in the store is on sale at prices that range from 30 – 50% off. Lots
of outerwear, ski suits, children's snowsuits and of course skis and boards. We
saw a great jacket for $99. Skiers and boarders will recognise names like
Couloir, Metropolis, Ripzone, Misty Mountain and more. Sale is ongoing until
new spring merchandise arrives. Historic Unionville is a lovely place to
browse and shop, so make it an outing!
170 Main Street (north off Hwy 7 just west of Kennedy Rd.), Unionville.
Tel: 905-513-0442
Hours: Monday to Friday 10 a.m. to 9 p.m., Saturday 10 a.m. to 6 p.m.,
Sunday 11:30 a.m. to 5:30 p.m.

SI VOUS PLAY SPORTS

With four stores and a clearance centre, this small chain offers name brand Athletic footwear and apparel such as Nike, Adidas, Fila, Reebok, Avirex, Ocean Pacific and Phat Farm. Prices are regularly 20-60% off the retail price with new arrivals weekly.

(Warehouse Outlet) 6931 Steeles Ave. W. (west of Hwy. 27), Rexdale.
Tel: 416-675-9235
Hours: W. to F. 10 - 9, Sat. 10 – 6
Lawrence Square, 700 Lawrence Ave. W., Toronto.
Tel: 416-256-1501
Hours: M. to F. 10 - 9, Sat. 10 – 6
Westwood Mall, 7205 Goreway Dr., Malton.
Tel: 905-677-4596
Hours: M. to F. 10 - 9, Sat. 10 – 6
York Gate Mall, 1 York Gate Blvd. (north west corner of Jane St. and Finch Ave.), North York.
Tel: 416-650-5665
Hours: M. to F. 10 - 9, Sat. 10 – 6
902 Simcoe St. N., Unit # 1, Oshawa.
Tel: 905-725-3339
Hours: M. to F. 10-8, Sat. 10-6

See advertisement on page A23

SILENT SPORTS - BICYCLING/ WINDSURFING/ SNOWBOARDING/ CROSS COUNTRY SKIING OUTLET

Bicycling/ Windsurfing/ Snowboarding/ Cross Country Skiing enthusiasts - check this out. They guarantee best value and satisfaction with stock that will boggle the technical types.

113 Doncaster Ave., Thornhill.
Tel: 905 - 889-3772 or 1-800-661-7873
Hours: M. to W. 10 - 6, Thu. & F. 10 - 9, Sat. 10 - 6
(May - July - Sundays 12 - 5)

sportwear and gear

SPORTS WORLD 🎒
Full line of Nordic and alpine skis, snowboards and exercise equipment.
Be sure to get on their mailing list for the Sept., Jan. and March sales to take
advantage of seasonal sales which include inline skates, exercise equipment and
much more.

> 89 Doncaster Ave. (first lights north of Yonge St.), Thornhill.
> Tel: 905-707-7368
> Hours: Fri. 9 -8; Sat. 9 - 6; Sun. 11 - 5.
> Call or e-mail: dwg@idirect.com for sale dates and to get on their
> mailing list.

SPORTSWAP

> 2063 Yonge Street (between Eglinton Ave. and Davisville Ave.), Toronto.
> Tel: 416-481-0249
> Hours: M. to F. 10 - 9, Sat. 9 - 6, Sun. 11 - 6

SUNGLASS SAFARI 🎒
There's no better time to buy a great pair of sunglasses at terrific prices. This
outlet has over half a million dollars in inventory to clear out with discontinued styles, samples and overstocks. Brand names include Serengeti, Ray Ban,
Reebok, DKNY, Hilfiger, Bollé and lots more. Prices will range from 25 - 75%
off - warranty on all products. Wheelchair accessible.

> Location: 2601 Matheson Blvd. E., unit #3 (just north of Centennial Park
> near Renforth and Eglinton), Etobicoke.
> Tel: 905-629-8333 or 1 - 800 - 263-0100 (Call for sale date)
> Hours: Weekdays noon to 7 pm, Saturdays and Sundays 11 - 4

See advertisement on page 66

Pharmacist - A helper on the farm.

---

personal and healthcare products

ACTION INVENTORY WAREHOUSE SALE - 🏷️

We cannot mention the brand names, but you will find all the popular brands here at this cosmetic and fragrance sale. Lots of bath and sun products as well as many gift sets, candles, watches and of course, fragrances at up to 80% off regular price. Five days only.

131 Don Park Road, (east off Woodbine Ave., north of Steeles Ave.), Markham.

Tel: 905-474-0188 Call for 2002-3 sale date.

Hours: Wednesday to Friday noon to 8 p.m., Saturday 11 a.m. to 5 p.m., and Sunday 11 a.m. to 5 p.m.

BEAUTY CLUB

1170 Bay St. (south of Bloor St.), Toronto.

Tel: 416-929-2582

Hours: M. to W. 10 - 6, Thu. & F. 10 - 7, Sat. 9 – 5

Call for other locations.

BEAUTY SUPPLY OUTLETS

769 Yonge St., Toronto

Tel: 416-934-0911

Call for other locations.

BELVEDERE INTERNATIONAL WAREHOUSE SALE 🏷️

The holiday season just wouldn't be the same without Belvedere International's 10-Day Christmas sale. Brand name hair care products and other toiletries are their mainstay, but there are also great deals on Christmas wrapping paper, decorations, and gift sets for men and women. You'll also find an amazing selection of toys for all ages, an assortment of leather purses, backpacks, wallets and designer fragrances. There is something for everyone on your list at this sale.

5640 Kennedy Rd. (Hwy. #401 west to Hwy. #10, south to Matheson Blvd., east on Matheson to Kennedy Rd.), Mississauga.

Tel: 905-568-4556.

Hours: Call for sale dates. Weekdays 11:00 a.m. - 8:00 p.m., Weekends 9-6.

personal and healthcare products

THE BODY SHOP
Canada One Factory Outlet, 7500 Lundy's Lane, Niagara Falls.
Tel: 905-371-2810
Call for other locations.

CLEARANCE WAREHOUSE
10 Bramhurst Avenue, Unit 3 and 4 (second light north of Steeles Ave. off Torbram Road), Brampton.
Tel: 905-799-1694
Hours: M. to F. 9-8, S. - S. 9-6

COSMETICS 'N' MORE
Cookstown Manufacturer's Outlet Mall, (south east corner of Hwy. 89 and Hwy. 400), Cookstown.
Tel: 705- 458-4193.
Hours: M. to F. 10-9, Sat. to Sun. 9-6

COSMETICS WAREHOUSE INC.
Save on top designer fragrances for that special Valentine. Many to choose from including Christian Dior, Versace, Lancome, Gucci, Elizabeth Taylor, and Fendi. We picked up a great Swiss Army gift set for our Valentine regularly $65 for $30 and Perry Ellis Reserve regularly $50 for $25. You'll also find real bargains on highend cosmetics including Revlon and L'Oreal.

275 Queen St.East (2 blocks west of Hwy. 410), Brampton
1355 Kingston Road, Pickering Town Centre; 700 Lawrence Ave. West, Lawrence Square Shopping Centre; 208 Apex road (Lawrence and Dufferin Ave.), Toronto.
Perfumery Oshawa Centre
419 King St. W., (across from Chapters).
Tel: 905 - 436-9904
Hours: Mon. to Fri. 10:30 - 8:00; Sat.10 - 6; Sunday noon to 5

See advertisement on page A12

personal and healthcare products

DAREE/GIFT-PAK WAREHOUSE SALE - 🎁

Hard to believe this is their 10th warehouse sale, and that we were at the first one! As always, you'll find great gift ideas and stocking stuffers for the entire family at up to 70% off. Cosmetics, hair products, gloves, food items, and even handmade chocolate pizzas at 40% off retail. Great hostess gift ideas for about the same price as a bottle of wine. As well, if you like creating your own gift baskets, they have just about everything you can possibly need at wholesale prices.

    5486 Gorvan Drive (west of Dixie Road, north of Matheson Rd.), Mississauga.
    Tel: 905-624-3359
    Hours: Call for sale dates. Monday to Friday 9:00 a.m. to 5:00 p.m. (7:00 pm on Thursday), Saturday 10:00 a.m. to 4:00 p.m. Closed Sunday

See advertisement on page A8

DESIGNER FRAGRANCES - OFF-PRICES PERFUMES
    5635 Finch Ave. East, Unit 2, Toronto.
    Tel: 416-754-2693
    Hours: M. to W. 10 - 7, Thu. 10 - 8, F. 10 - 8, Sat. 10 - 6, Sun. 12 - 5

GIFT-PAK 🎁

This distributor of gourmet goods and basket supplies has everything for the do-it-yourself basket-maker; fine food, imported chocolate, candles and glassware, bath and baby products, baskets, designer ribbon and bows....ALL AT WHOLESALE PRICES ! Save up to 50 %. Great ideas for loot bags, bombonieres, teacher gifts, stocking stuffers, hostess gifts and hard-to-buy-for people on your list. Enjoy additional savings during their November and April Warehouse Sales (held along with their sister company Daree Imports and Sales Ltd.).

    5486 Gorvan Drive, (south of Hwy. 401, go east off Tomken Rd. onto Brevik Place and left onto Gorvan Dr.), Mississauga.
    Tel: 905-624-9560
    Hours: M. to W. & F. 9-4, Thur. 9-7, Sat. 10-3
    (Closed Sat. in the summer)

See advertisement on page A8

personal and healthcare products

LISA'S COSMETICS WAREHOUSE SALE 🎁

Here you can find a gift for everyone on Santa's list. There are men's and ladies fine fragrances from Gucci, Swiss Army, White Diamonds, Versace Red Jeans/Blue Jeans,
Halston, Fendi, Royal Doulton and many more. The savings are up to 80% off regular prices. You'll also be able to pick up name brand cosmetics. This sale only runs for 16 days so pick up Christmas gifts and stocking stuffers for everyone on your list.

> 8555 Woodbine Ave. (corner Woodbine Ave. and Hwy. #7, formerly Knob Hill Farms), Markham
> Tel: 905-886-6528
> Hours: Call to confirm location and for sale date and hours.

MARKHAM VITAMIN WAREHOUSE OUTLET - NUTRITIONAL PRODUCTS 🎁

Inside this large, spacious store is a huge selection of vitamins, nutritional products, cereals, beauty aids and more - at prices lower than most of the smaller health stores. Swiss Herbal Remedies are always 30% off suggested retail prices. Granola bars and cereals are also discounted. Once a year this 4000 foot store clears out inventory which includes vitamins, sports nutrition products, natural foods, herbal and homeopathic products. For one week only, all items in the store will be 10-50% less than their already low prices.

> 330 Steelecase Rd. E. (east of Hwy. 404), south of Denison St.), Markham.
> Tel: 905-475-5366
> Hours: M. to Sat. 10 - 6 (Call for sale date(s).
> See advertisement on page A12

MASSAGE THERAPY CLINIC - CENTENNIAL COLLEGE

Here's something to help soothe the aching muscles - especially if you've been shopping all day! This three year program includes as part of the curriculum a clinic where you can experience a wonderful relaxing massage for only $25. The one hour clinic includes an assessment by the student, so be prepared to discuss any specific areas you would like the staff to work on. (Opens 1st Tuesday after Labour Day)
Centennial College, Warden Woods Campus (Warden Avenue south of St. Clair Ave.), Scarborough. The clinic is held in the Annex, with an entrance right

personal and healthcare products

off Warden Ave., Scarborough. Look for the signs.
Tel: 416-289-5353
Hours: 3rd Year Clinic, T. & Thu. (relaxation & rehabilitation treatment of musculoskeletal problems);
2nd Year Clinic, M., W., F. (focus on stress management and relaxation).
Call for appointments daily - 12:30, 2:00, 4:30 and 6:00 pm.

MR. B'S "FAMOUS" WAREHOUSE SALE 🛍

Six Sales per year: March, May, July, September, October, December. Every Sale is unique in merchandise and theme but the constant thread throughout is National Brands at below wholesale prices. This is a department store mix in a warehouse environment. Children welcome; Fun & Excitement Provided. Products include: Sunglasses, Reading Glasses, Cosmetics, Personal Care, Fragrances, Soaps, Shampoo, Hair care, Hair Accessories, Personal Appliances, Household, Clothing, Videos, CD's, Tapes, Candles, Pot Pourri, Health and Fitness, Fashion Jewelry. Visa - Interac - Shopping Carts - Free Parking
Their slogan is "Rock your Socks Prices"........ Believe It!.
1590 Matheson Blvd. Unit #12. (East of Dixie Rd., south of Matheson Blvd E.) Mississauga.
Tel: 905-629-1500
Hours: Mon-Fri 11 until 8, Sat-Sun 10 until 4

See advertisement on page A22

PERFUME GALORE

1333 Kennedy Rd. Scarborough.
Tel: 416-750-4619
Hours: M. to F., 10-9, Sat. 10-6, Sun. 12-5.
Call for other location.

PROCTOR & GAMBLE 🛍

Numerous brand name products from Procter & Gamble will be available at this sale. Included as well will be Cover Girl, Olay, and Max Factor cosmetics. Prices are always excellent, and stock tends to change from sale to sale depending on product availability.
Great for stocking up on products for the cottage like facial tissue and toilet paper!
Call for location and dates.
Tel: 1-800-668-0198

personal and healthcare products

QHP/TRESSES - QUALITY HAIR PRODUCTS OUTLET
1923 Avenue Rd. (south of Wilson Ave.), Toronto.
Tel: 416-787-0141
Hours: M. to F. 9:30 - 8, Sat. & Sun. 9 - 6

REVLON WAREHOUSE SALE 🏠
Just in time for Christmas gift giving, a huge warehouse sale of Revlon, Almay, plus special products from the U.S. Great deals on fragrances, cosmetics, beauty care and more, up to 80% off.
Also, visit the company store which is open to public.
Call 905-276-4500 ext. 273

See advertisement on page A19

VIDAL SASSOON SALON
37 Avenue Rd. (two blocks north of Bloor St. at Yorkville Ave.), Toronto.
Tel: 416-920-0593
Hours: M. to F. 9:30 - 5, Call to book an appointment
613- 236-9731

Bible revisions by minors
Actual responses to bible questions on a test given to elementary school kids.

•In the first book of the bible, Guinessis, God got tired of creating the world, so he took the Sabbath off.

•Adam and Eve were created from an apple tree.

•Noah's wife was called Joan of Ark. Noah built an ark, which the animals came on to in pears.

---

food fair and wine

ALMOST PERFECT THRIFT FROZEN FOODS AND MORE

When you are doing all your shopping and don't have time for cooking, these three outlets can save the day. They carry a huge variety of foods – frozen, refrigerated and confectionary. Pick up everything you need for holiday entertaining from steaks and chicken, pizza, pasta and hors d'oeuvres, cakes, pies and ice cream, cookies, seafood and breads all generally at savings 30% to 50% off regular retail, and sometimes more. Lots of specials and the selection changes almost daily. Two wheelchair accessible locations.

919 Bloor St. E, (between Ritson Rd. & Simcoe St.), Oshawa.
Tel: 905-434-1111
180 Harwood Ave. S. (in the Ajax Plaza), Ajax .
Tel: 905-683-1111
1150 Sheppard Ave. W., (Allan Rd. & Sheppard Ave.), Toronto.
Tel: 416-222-1111.
Hours: Monday to Wednesday 10 a.m. to 6 p.m., Thursday and
Friday 10 a.m. to 8 p.m., Saturday 10 a.m. to 6 p.m., Sunday noon to 5 p.m.

AMADEUS - FINE CAKES LTD.

7380 Bathurst St. (north of Steeles Ave.), Thornhill.
Tel: 905-882-9957
Hours: M. to Sat. 8 - 10, Sun. 8 - 9

ARCHIBALD ORCHARDS & ESTATE WINERY

6275 Liberty Street North, R.R #5, Bowmanville. Take 401 to Liberty
Street exit North to Taunton Road - right hand side
Tel: 905 - 263-2396
Hours: 9 – 6 seven days a week

AUNT SARAH'S - CANDY FACTORY OUTLET

140 Doncaster Ave., Unit 1, Thornhill.
Tel: 905-731-3900
Hours: Call for store hours.

BAKER'S HOUSE

1774 Drew Rd., Mississauga.
Tel: 905-676-1077
Hours: M. to F. 9 - 6:30, Sat. 10 - 5

food fair and wine

BETA BRANDS LIMITED

Better known as McCormicks, this outlet store carries a wide variety of bulk candy and crackers. We bought all sorts of things to try – Life-Savers, Ju Jubes,, bridge mixture, cherry blasters – and found them to be exceptionally fresh and very well priced. They also sell some products by the 10 kg box at downright ridiculous prices, so if you are planning a large event, or a children's party you might want to consider dropping in next time you're in London.

1156 Dundas Street E. (just west of Highbury Ave.), London.
Tel: 519-455-2250
Hours: Monday to Friday 8:30 a.m. to 5 p.m., Saturday 9 a.m. to 4 p.m.

BILLY BEE HONEY PRODUCTS LTD.

This has to be the smallest outlet we've previewed! Inside the front lobby is a wall with shelves, and some of the best deals around on this well known, brand name honey. The product varies and includes honeyed nuts, honey mustard and honey garlic sauce, as well as pails of honey. They do offer factory tours, which would make an inexpensive outing for Guides, Scouts, schools etc. Cash only.

8 Tycos Drive, (west off Dufferin St., south of Lawrence Ave.), Toronto.
Tel: 416 -789-4391
Hours: M. to F. 9 - 4:30

BONCHEFF GREENHOUSES

Fresh salads and veggies are bound to be on your menu this weekend, so a visit to this greenhouse may be in order. They carry a wonderful selection of baby vegetables and French green beans, as well as a full range of fresh herbs at $1.00/bunch, California spring mix and baby spinach . Prices are excellent, and produce is always fresh.

382 Olivewood Road (south of Bloor St. W. between Islington Ave. and Kipling Ave.), Toronto.
Tel: 416-233-6922
Hours: Monday to Friday 8:00 a.m. to 4:00 p.m., Saturday 9:00 a.m. to 4:00 p.m.

food fair and wine

CADBURY OUTLET STORE
Cookstown Manufacturer's Outlet Mall at Hwy 400 and Hwy 89.
Tel: 705-458-4666
Hours: M. to F. 10- 9, Sat., Sun., and Holidays 10 - 6.
Call for other locations.

CAMPBELL'S SOUP FACTORY OUTLET
1400 Mitchell Road South. (Hwy. 23, about 1 km south of Listowel
Located inside a portable in the parking lot.).
Tel: 519-291-3410
Hours: Tues., W. & Sat. 9 - 5, Thu. 9 - 8, F. 9 - 6

CANADIAN HICKORY FARMS 🏠
107 Corstat Avenue,
Concord
Tel: 905-669-5929
Mail orders: 1-800-845-4464
Web site: www.hickoryfarm.ca
Hours: M. to F. 10 - 5, Sat. 10 – 4, Closed Sun.

CARDINAL MEAT FACTORY OUTLET
2396 Stanfield Rd., (N. of The Queensway between Cawthra Rd. and Dixie
Rd.), Mississauga.
Tel: 905-279-1734
Hours: M. to F. 9:30 - 5:30, Sat. 9 - 5, Sun 10:30 - 4:30

CILENTO WINES
672 Chrislea Dr. (just north of Hwy. #7, east of Weston Rd.), Woodbridge.
Tel: 905 264-9463
Hours: M.- Fri. 9 -7, Sat. to 6, Sun. 11 - 5

Avoidable - What a bull fighter tries to do.

---

food fair and wine

CJay DISTRIBUTORS

Gourmet Teas, Macy's Cheese sticks, Spicy Bites, tea accessories and gift packages for all occasions. Nothing better than a good cup of tea.....so if you really enjoy tea, drop into this outlet which features a wide selection of black and green tea, herbal tea and Masala Chai in both tea leaves and tea bags. These teas are imported directly from the great tea gardens from around the world and blended and packed in Canada. They also carry a wide variety of award winning Macy's Cheese sticks. Right now many of the items are up to 50% off retail prices.

> 70 Don Park Road, Unit 4 (off Denison St., North of Steeles Ave., east of Woodbine Ave.), Markham.
> Tel: 905-947-0444
> Hours: Regular hours M.-F. 10 to 3, Sat. 11 to 2

DAVID ROBERTS FOOD CORPORATION 🏢

What would Christmas be without wonderful goodies? This annual sale brings freshly roasted nuts, candy, gourmet chocolates and biscuits at substantially reduced prices. Their jumbo cashews are a bargain at $4.99 for a 400 gram tub, and the chocolate almonds are also bargain priced for the sale. Ready made, Gourmet gift baskets are offered at 25-50% off their regular prices.

> 426 Watline Avenue (sw corner at Kennedy Road, north of Matheson Blvd.), Mississauga.
> Tel: 905-502-7700

See advertisement on page A30

DIANA'S SEAFOOD WHOLESALE FISH DISTRIBUTORS

> 2101 Lawrence Avenue E., Scarborough.
> Tel: 416-288-9286
> Hours: M. & Sat. 9 – 6, T. - F. 9 – 7, Sun. 10 - 5

Baloney - Where some hemlines fall.

DEL'S PASTRY LTD.

A delightful aroma greets you as you enter this bakery outlet, stocked fresh daily with muffins, tea biscuits, pies, cookies and buns. During the Christmas season, they have wonderful specials on Christmas goodies that include mince meat tarts, shortbread cookies and wonderful German loaf cakes. Their chocolate chip cookies are also great! Drop in to visit, and you just may not need to bake!

344 Bering Ave., (between Kipling Ave. and Islington Ave. north of The Queensway), Toronto.
Tel: 416-231-4383
Hours: M. to F. 7 - 6, Sat. 8 - 3

See advertisement on page A10

DIMPFLMEIER BAKERY OUTLET

26-36 Advance Road (south of Bloor St. between Kipling Ave. and Islington Ave.), Etobicoke.
Tel: 416 -239-3031
Hours: M. to F. 7 - 9, Sat. 8 - 6, Sun. 9 - 5

DONINI'S CHOCOLATE OUTLET - FACTORY OUTLET

335 Bell Blvd., Belleville.

DOVER FLOUR MILLS

140 King St. W., Cambridge.
Tel: 19- 653-6267
Hours: M. to F. 9 - 5

Paradox - Two physicians.

food fair and wine

DOWNEY'S MARKET FARM

Looking for a pumpkin? Pumpkins are by the 1000's here and priced from 75 cents up according to size. This is an ultimate family Halloween outing and headquarters for all your haunting needs. Take the kids into the new Boo-barn or decorate a pumpkin to take home. There is also a petting farm, pony rides and Ontario's largest goat walk. While you are there, pick up some wonderful farm fresh produce, pumpkin pies and baked goods.

> 13682 Heart Lake Road (Hwy. 410 north to Heartlake Rd) Inglewood,
> Tel: 905-838-2990.
> Hours: 9 a.m. to 6 p.m. daily

EGLI'S MEAT MARKET

> 162 Snider Rd. E., Baden.
> Tel: 19- 634-5320
> Hours: Tues. & W. 8 - 5, Thu. 8 - 5:30, F. 8 - 6, Sat. 8 - 2

EMPIRE ORCHARDS & HERB FARM

> Taunton Road, East of Hwy. 57, (401 to Bowmanville, north to
> Taunton Road and turn right).
> Tel: 905-263-8161
> Hours: 10-6 - 7 days a week

EUROPEAN CHEESECAKE FACTORY LTD.
(See WOW! Factor Desserts)

EUROPEAN QUALITY MEATS & SAUSAGES

Even though you need to take a number and wait your turn, the prices and quality of the meat products here make it all worthwhile. Specials this week include boneless chicken breasts at $3.49/lb., New York steaks at $5.49/lb. And baby back ribs at $4.99/lb. Their prices are always competitive, with lots of selection.

> 16 Jutland Ave. (north of the Queensway, west of Islington Ave.), Toronto.
> Tel: 416-251-6193
> Hours: Monday , Wednesday and Saturday 8 a.m. to 6 p.m., Thursday and
> Friday until 7 p.m.
> 176 Baldwin Street (Kensington Market, north of Dundas St.), Toronto.
> Tel: 416-596-8691
> Hours: Monday, Wednesday and Saturday 8 a.m. to 7 p.m., Thursday until
> 8p.m., Friday until 9 p.m.

---

food fair and wine

FOOD DEPOT INTERNATIONAL

This delightful shop brims with European delicacies, coffee, biscuits and canned goods. Best of all is their fresh cheese, which is always competitively priced and exceptionally fresh. If you love to make raclette as we do, their raclette cheese is second to none. And try their truffles, which are an exceptional treat.

> 14 Jutland Rd. (north of The Queensway, west off Islington Ave.), Etobicoke.
> Tel: 416 -253-5257
> Hours: M. to Sat. 9 - 6

FUTURE BAKERY

Dizzying arrays of rye breads, Kyivan, poppyseed and caraway, focacias, ciabattas, whole wheat, San Francisco sourdough breads - in all 28 different assortments of breads for your Easter table at priced at factory low prices.
We also picked up some wonderful fruit marmalades at 3 for $2.98 and a large jar of roasted, peeled red peppers for only $1.99. Be sure to drop in here for all your Easter dinner accessories.

> 106 North Queen Street (north of The Queensway, east of The East Mall), Etobicoke.
> Tel: 416-231-1491
> Hours: M-F., 8 - 8; Sat. 8 - 6 Sun 9 -5

G. BRANDT MEAT PACKERS

> 1878 Mattawa Ave., (between Dixie Rd. and Hwy. 427, south of Dundas St.), Mississauga.
> Tel: 905-279-4460
> Hours: M. to W. 8 - 6, Th. Fr. 8 – 7, Sat. 7 - 2

GRANDE CHEESE COMPANY - FACTORY OUTLETS

> 175 Milvan Dr., Weston.
> Tel: 416-740-8883
> Hours: M. to F. 3 - 6, Sat 8 - 5, Sun. 9 - 3
> Call for other locations.

food fair and wine

HERSHEY CANADA INC.

1 Hershey Dr. (take Hwy. 401 east to Kingston, then Hwy. 15 north to
Smiths Falls, follow the signs to the outlet), Smiths Falls.
Tel: 13-283-3300
Hours: M. to F. 9 - 6, Sat. 9 - 5, Sun. 10 - 5

HONOR'S PASTRIES

1085 Bellamy Rd. N.. Unit 22 (north of Ellesmere Rd), Scarborough.
Tel: 416-439-6031
Hours: Tues. to Thu. 12 - 5, F. 12 - 6:30, Sat. 11 - 4

KRUG'S MEAT MARKET

28 Woodstock St., Tavistock.
Tel: 519- 655-2221
Hours: M. to F. 7 - 6, Sat. 7 - 3

LAURA SECORD OUTLET STORES

Canada's premiere chocolatier since 1913 has two outlet locations in the
Toronto area. The two stores offer slightly imperfect chocolates and out of
season candies at greatly reduced prices. They taste just as good, but cost a
whole lot less. While you are there, also pick up some Laura Secord's premi-
um ice cream. Everything is made out of the finest ingredients using recipes
the company has had for over 85 years.
Warden Power Centre, 725 Warden Avenue, Scarborough
Tel:416-615-1677
Dixie Outlet Mall, 1250 South Service Road, Mississauga.
Tel: 905 - 271-1433.
Hours: Monday to Friday 10 a.m. to 9 p.m. Saturday 9:30 a.m. to 6 p.m.
Sunday noon to 5 p.m. (Dixie until 6 p.m.)

LCBO CLEARANCE CENTRE 🛒

What better time than prior to the long weekend to pick up some bargains at
the LCBO of all places! At this clearance location you'll find mainly wine that
is going to be delisted, or there's not enough to keep in stock in their regular
stores. Prices are generally 10-20% off regular prices and occasionally you can
find some real deals.
625 Weston Road (in the Crossroads Centre), Toronto.
Tel: 416-243-3320
Call for sale date(s) and hours.

MAPLEHURST BAKERY OUTLET

This outlet carries the complete line of Sara Lee cake and pastry products at discounted prices. Savings fluctuate depending on inventory levels. It is mainly seconds that are sold in the outlet locations, but there is nothing wrong with either the quality or the ingredients; generally they have been classified as seconds because of minor cosmetic glitches! Cash only.

379 Orenda Road, Brampton
Tel: 905 - 791-3147
Hours: Monday to Friday 9:30 to 5 - Saturday 9-5.

MAPLE LODGE FARMS LTD.

Purchase fresh and frozen chicken at wholesale prices. It's really the chicken they're best known for. Be prepared to buy in large quantities either by the case or in 5 kg bags. A 25-pound case of chicken legs, backs attached, is 55 cents/pound - so shop with a friend.

8301 Winston Churchill Blvd. (Hwy. 401 west to Winston Churchill Blvd. and north over Steeles Ave.), Brampton.
Tel: 905-455-8340
Hours: Open all year, but only open weekends July and August.
Sat. 10 to 5, Sunday noon to 5

MAPLE ORCHARD FARMS & THE CHOCOLATE FACTORY

14 Gray Rd, Bracebridge.
Tel: 705-645-3053
Hours: Open year round, but only on weekends during July and August.
Sat. 10 - 5; Sun. 12 - 5; Balance of year: M. to F. 9 - 4:30; Sat/Sun, same as July/Aug.

McCORMICKS FACTORY OUTLET STORE

1156 Dundas Street (two blocks west of Highbury Ave.), London.
Tel: 19- 455-2250
Hours: M. to F. 8:30 - 5:00, Sat. 9:30 - 4:00

food fair and wine

MARKHAM WAREHOUSE OUTLET- 🏢
NUTRITIONAL PRODUCTS

Inside this large store is a hugh selection of vitamins, nutritional products, cereals, beauty aids, and more - at prices lower than most of the smaller health food stores. Swiss Herbal Remedies are always 30% off suggested retail pricees. Granola bars and cereals are also discounted. Once a year this 4,000 foot store clears out inventory which includes vitamines, sports nutrition products, natural foods, herbal and homeopathic products. For one day only, all items in the store will be 10-50% less than their already low prices. Call for sale dates and hours.

> 330 Steelcase Rd., E. (east of Hwy 404) south of Denison St., Markham.
> Tel: 905-475-5366
> Hours: M.-Sat. 10-6.

See advertisement on page A12

NABISCO/CHRISTIE FACTORY OUTLET STORES

> 370 Progress Avenue (south of the 401, west of Brimley Road), Scarborough.
> Tel: 416-291-3713
> Hours: M. to F. 8:30 - 4:30
> Call for other locations.

NATIONAL CHEESE COMPANY LTD.

> 675 Rivermede Rd., Concord.
> Tel: 905-669-9393
> Hours: M. to F. 8:30 - 5, Sat. 8 - 5, Sun. 8 - 1

OAK GROVE CHEESE FACTORY - OUTLET STORE

> 29 Bleams Rd. E. (north off Hwy. 7/8 on to Peel St.), New Hamburg.
> Tel: 19- 662-1212
> Hours: M. to F. 9 - 5, Sat. 9 - 1

PASTA INTERNATIONAL

> 5715 Coopers Ave., Unit 8 (north of Matheson Blvd. and east off Kennedy Rd.), Mississauga.
> Tel: 905-890-5550
> Hours: M. to F. 9 - 5:30

PASTA QUISTINI
551 Jevlan Drive (Hwy 400 and Hwy. 7), Woodbridge.
Tel: 905-851-2030
Hours: M-F. 8 - 5:30, Sat. 10 - 2:30

PASTACO INC. FRESH NOODLES AND PASTA PRODUCTS
1140 Sheppard Ave. West, Unit 14, Downsview.
Tel: 416-630-3635
Hours: M. to F. 8:30 to 6, Sat. 9 to 5

PFALZGRAF CANADA INC.
90 Saunders Rd., Units 4 -6, Barrie.
Tel: 705-739-8980
Hours: M. to F. 8 - 6

PINGLE'S FARM MARKET
1805 Taunton Road East
401 East - Exit 425 to Courtise Road (east of Oshawa)
South east corner of Taunton Road and Courtise.
Tel: 905-725-6089
Hours: M.- F. 8-7; Sat. & Sun 8-6.

PREMIER BRANDS WAREHOUSE SALE 🏢
For anyone on your list who has a sweet tooth, be sure to visit this warehouse sale. You'll find manufacturer's prices cut by one third with most items
in the $1 to $10 range. There is something for everyone's pocket including
premium European chocolates, European biscuits, shortbread gift boxes, cookies, stocking fillers, bars, gift tins, chutney and jams. Cash only
1380 Birchmount Rd (N. of Lawrence Ave.), Toronto.
Tel: 416-750-8807
Hours: Call for sale dates. M.-F. 10:00 a.m. - 6:00 p.m., Sat.y 10:00 a.m. -
5:00 p.m., Sun. 11:00 a.m. - 4:00 p.m.

food fair and wine

QZINA FACTORY CLEARANCE

110 Woodbine Downs Blvd. Unit #3 (Carrier Dr & Hwy 27, North of Finch Avenue), Etobicoke.
Tel: 416-675-2282
Hours: Call for sale dates and hours.

REINHARDT FOOD – FACTORY OUTLET

214 King St. N., (northwest corner at Hwy. 26 and Airport Rd.), Stayner.
Tel: 705-428-2422
Call for a price list.
Hours: Office is open M. to F. 8-5 for ordering, with pick ups on Tuesday or Thursday.

ROYCE DUPONT

This name has been synonymous with quality poultry products for years in Toronto. In fact for over 70 years the same family has run this business. With a wide variety of poultry products that include duck, quail, Cornish hens and chicken, you're sure to find something to whet your family's appetite. Their chicken is "air chilled" which results in a plumper, juicier chicken. We tried their Cornish hens which were $4.29 each and weighed at least one and a half pounds – they were delicious. As well, they'll smoke a turkey for you the old fashioned way right on the premises – a great idea for your next party.

1507 Dupont Street (at the corner of Symington Ave.), Toronto
Tel: 416-534-2323
Hours: Monday to Saturday 8 a.m. to 6 p.m.

SEAFOOD DEPOT

81 Aviva Park Dr., Woodbridge.
Tel: 905-856-2770 or
Toll free: 1-800-563-6222
Hours: M. & Sat. 8 - 5, T. & W. 9 - 6, Thu. 9 - 7, Fri. 8 - 8.

SIENA FOODS/COLIO WINES - OUTLET STORE

2300 Haines Rd. (north of the Queensway between Cawthra and Dixie Rds.), Mississauga.
Tel: 05-949-4246
Hours: M. to F., 9: 30 - 6, Sat. 9 - 5

---

food fair and wine

SIMON'S SMOKEHOUSE - FACTORY OUTLET

220 Clarence St. (between Steeles Ave. and Queen St., east of Kennedy Rd.), Brampton.
Tel: 905-453-1822
Hours: M. to W. 9 - 5, Thu. & F. 9 – 7, Sat. 9-5

THE HUMBLE PIE

6 Bay Street, next door to the liquor store, just off Hwy. 117 as you pass through Baysville.
Tel: 705-767-1136.
Hours: Open most weekends, with irregular hours during the week

THE SALAD KING

896 Lakeshore Rd. E. (between Dixie and Cawthra Rds.), Mississauga.
Tel: 905-891-1912
Hours: M. to F. 9-5 (Summer hours open Sat. 9 - 1)

TOMEK'S NATURAL PRESERVES

This tiny outlet carries great specialty food products, which are homemade and very fresh. We tried the dill pickles and thought they were terrific, and husband Brian who loves herring pronounced it one of the best ever. Dill pickles are $3.39/kilo, sauerkraut is $2.20/kilo and perogies are $2.99/dozen. Red and white borscht is ready to eat and reasonably priced at $2.50 for a large jar. Maybe your mother in law will think you cooked all day!

9 Advance Road (south of Bloor St. between Kipling Ave. and Islington Ave.), Etobicoke.
Tel: 416-234-1943
Hours: M. to F. 8-6, Sat. 8-4, Closed Sun.

Misty - How golfers create divots.

TRE MARI BAKERY - FACTORY OUTLET

This commercial bakery has an outlet on the premises that sells overruns from the day. All products are fresh and selection varies daily. Advance notice is required for large orders. Cash only.

41 Shorncliffe Rd. (south off Dundas St. and west of Kipling Ave.), Etobicoke.

Tel: 416-233-3800

Hours: M. to Sat. 9 - 6, Sun. 10 - 4

TYRONE MILLS LIMITED

2656 Concession #7, Bowmanville.

401 East to Liberty Street go north approximately 10 miles.

Hours: M.-Sat., 9-6; Sun. noon-5.

VINOTECA PREMIUM WINERY

For over 13 years, this Canadian winery has produced many different varietal wines at bulk prices. An 18 litre pail starts at $85.00. Founded in 1989, Vinoteca is a family winery offering fine quality VQA and varietal wines at competitive prices. Many medals awarded in prestigious competitions are on display, including gold and silver medals for their icewines. We dropped in and sampled both white and red wines available in bottles, boxes and pails. These pails are great value for the cottage or a party and are refundable, returnable and recyclable. Vinoteca is one of the few wineries to offer complimentary private labeling for special personal, family, and corporate events, such as weddings, anniversaries etc. Wine tastings, winery tours and great gift ideas make the drive to Woodbridge well worthwhile. They also have their own vineyards in the Niagara Peninsula and Italy.

527 Jevlan Drive, Woodbridge, Ont. (East of Weston Rd., North of #7 Hwy.)

Tel: 905-856-5700; toll Free: 1-866-313-5700

Web Site: www.toronto.com/vinoteca

Canada Post Delivery is now available.

See advertisement on page 96

food fair and wine

VITAL LINK ICE CREAM SALE

For the warm summer days that are approaching, this warehouse sale is the best place to find some special treats that the whole family will love. Save up to 50% off the retail price on name brand ice cream such as Nestle and Hagen Daz tubs of ice cream, frozen yogurts, novelties and ice cream desserts. Most of the products are in bulk so clear out your freezer to make room for these great bargains.

680 Petrolia Rd. (south west of the corner of Keel St. and Steeles Ave. W.) Downsview.

Tel: 416 663-5525

Hours: Call for sale date and hours.

food fair and wine

VOORTMAN COOKIES
4455 North Service Rd. (exit from the Q.E.W. at Appleby Line),
Burlington.
Tel: 905-335-9500
Hours: M. to F. 8:15 - 4:30

WESTON BAKERY OUTLET - FACTORY OUTLET STORE
1425 The Queensway (east of Hwy. 427), Etobicoke.
Tel: 416-252-7323
Hours: M. to F. 8 - 6, Sat. 8 – 5
Call for other locations.

WHAT A BASKET!
6705 Tomken Rd., Units 5 & 6 (Tomken & Derry Rds. area), Mississauga.
Tel: 905-670-8056
Hours: M. to F. 8:30 - 4:30, Sat. 10 – 3

WILD FLOWER FARM
R.R.#3 (between Schomberg & Nobleton on the first road W. of Hwy. 27,
just N. of the 17th Sideroad), Schomberg.
Tel: 905-859-0286
Hours: M. to Sun. 10 - 6

WILLIES MERCANTILE
236 Huron St., (turn south off Hwy. 26/Main St. at the TD Bank), Stayner.
Tel: 705-428-5722
Hours: M. to F. 9:30 - 5:30, Sat. 9-5, closed Mondays in Jan/Feb.

Left Bank - What the robber did when his bag was full of loot.

---

food fair and wine

WINE NOT

Wine Not is a full service, professional, on premises winemaking establishment dedicated to providing customers with the highest quality product, service and skill. They offer an extensive selection of red, white and specialty wines. Once you have selected and started your wine, their knowledgeable wine consultants monitor the fermentation process as the wine matures.

For those of you who have never experienced the fun of making your own wine, discover the Wine Not 2-step. Step 1 takes 5 minutes to choose your wine and start the fermentation process. For step 2, you return 4-6 weeks later to bottle your very own vintage. It's fun, fast and easy. Labels, corks, shrink-wrap and all applicable taxes are included in your price.

Tel: Toll Free 1-888-946-3668 for the location nearest you.
Website: www.winenot.com; e-mail: globalwinenot.com

WHITE FEATHERS COUNTRY STORE

15 Ragland Road East - 401 north on Simcoe Street (about ten miles north of 401 exit), Oshawa.
Tel: 905-655-4752
Hours: M.-Sat- 8:30-6, Tues and Fri. 8:30-8

WOW! FACTOR DESSERTS

If it's your turn to host the family Thanksgiving, you'll love this outlet which features mouth-watering cheescakes, pies and cakes with no preservatives or chemicals. They normally sell to the restaurant trade, but you can purchase directly from them as well. We loved their three-layer "Pumpkin Perfection" cheesecake which serves fourteen people for $31.00.

110 Clairport Crescent, Unit 2 (south of Steeles Avenue off Albion Road), Etobicoke
Tel: 416-674-0606
Hours: Monday to Friday 8:30 a.m. to 5:00 pm

for your home

- **Homefurnishings & Appliances**
- **Home Decorating &**
  Housewares
- **Fabrics & Linens**

Ransom

home furnishings and appliances

ADVANCE FURNITURE LTD.

2500 Lawrence Ave. E., (both Advance and the Scarborough Door Factory are on the north side of Lawrence Ave. E., just west of Midland and accessed by going south under the east side of the bridge), Scarborough.
Tel: 416-757-2444
Hours: Weekdays 10-8:30, Sat. 9-5.

ANDERSON'S FINE FURNITURE

A high quality, good value store. Gary's floor sample sale was currently underway when we dropped in to buy a chair, and discovered wonderful prices on Mission furniture, as well as custom sofas at affordable prices. Lots of great accessories as well.

2100 Bloor St. W. (west of High Park and east of Runneymede Rd.), Toronto.
Tel: 416-762-2666
Hours: T. to Sat. 10 – 6, Sun. 11 -5.

See advertisement on page A2

ART IN IRON

Art in Iron manufactures a wide range of affordable, quality wrought iron products from beds to tables. They occasionally have an up to 50% off sale on tables and giftware.

291 Jane Street, (north of Bloor St.), Toronto.
Tel: 416-762-7777 (Call for sale dates)
Hours: Monday to Saturday 10 a.m. to 6 p.m., Sunday noon to 4 p.m.

BARRYMORE FURNITURE MANUFACTURER 🏠

Can you believe that this will be Barrymore's 83rd, anniversary sale! And their tradition of fine quality furniture hasn't changed in all this time. Guaranteed best prices of the year on customized furniture with your choice of fabrics, seat depth, firmness and shape of cushions.

1137 King Street West (King Street and Atlantic Ave., four blocks east of Dufferin Street), Toronto.
Tel: 416-532-2891
Hours: Call for dates and times

home furnishings and appliances

BARTOLINI DESIGN STUDIO

The selection of plaster or concrete items is huge and varied with great pricing. Choose from hundreds of different designs for birdbaths, fountains, garden statuary, planters, wall plaques and sconces, dining table bases, pedestals, gargoyles and cherubs. This is the actual factory and it certainly is an interesting trip.   December warehouse sale features over-runs, ends of line and seconds. Call for dates.

> 244 Brockport Drive, Unit 20 (First road west of Hwy 27 and north off Belfield Road), Etobicoke.
> Tel: 416-675-7249
> Hours: M. to F. 9:30 to 5:30. Call for Sat. hours.

THE BOMBAY COMPANY OUTLET STORE

The Bombay Company, selling classic and timeless furniture, prints and accessories, offers Special Purchase Outlet products along with discontinued and slightly damaged pieces of its British-inspired home furnishings at discounted prices year round. They are available at 35% or more off regular retail prices. The huge warehouse at Kennedy Rd., just north of Hwy. 401 in Mississauga also has a once-a-year warehouse sale that is to die for! August Warehouse Sale.

> Dixie Outlet Mall, 1250 South Service Rd. (Dixie Rd. and the Q.E.W.), Mississauga.
> Tel: 905 - 278-5259
> Hours: M. to F. 10 - 9, Sat. 10 - 6, Sun. 12 - 6

BOMBAY.

OUTLET STORE

Discover fabulous finds in classic and timeless furniture, prints and home accessories! Special Purchase Outlet product along with discontinued, slightly damaged and/or overstocked home furnishings, all at wonderful prices!

DIXIE OUTLET MALL

1250 South Service Road, Mississauga
(Dixie Road and the QEW)

STORE HOURS: Monday - Friday 10am - 9pm
Saturday 9:30am - 6pm • Sunday 12 - 6pm
Tel: 905 - 278 - 5259

home furnishings and appliances

CAMCO INC. MAJOR APPLIANCES

This is a great opportunity with huge savings to pick up uncrated, end of line or scratch & dent appliances. Inventory includes GE, Hotpoint and Moffat major appliances. All come with a one year functional warranty.

5130 Dixie Road, Unit # 14 (401 hwy, to Dixie Road & South before Eglinton Ave, on the West side), Mississauga.

Tel: 905 - 602-5307

Hours: Monday to Friday 8:00am to 6:00pm, Saturday 9:00am to 5:00pm. OR check them out at www.ebay.ca/ge. Receive an additional 5% discount when purchasing on Ebay.ca

DANBY PRODUCTS -
APPLIANCES SCRATCH AND DENT WAREHOUSE SALE 🏠

5070 Whitelaw Rd.(Hwy. #24 and Whitelaw Rd. Hwy 401, N. on Hwy 6, west on Wellington St., right at 4th Stoplight), Guelph.

Tel: 519-837-0920

This annual sale is traditionally held on Mother's Day and is extremely popular. Call to confirm dates and times.

DECORIUM

363 Supertest Road (two lights north of Finch Ave. off Dufferin St.), North York.

Tel: 416-736-6120

Web site:www.decorium.ca

Hours: M.,T.,W., 10-6,Thu., Fri., 10-9, Sat. 10-6., Sun. noon to 5

DESIGNERS WALK GARAGE SALE 🏠

Designers Walk Bldg. #5, 160 Pears Ave. (one block north of Davenport Rd., go west off Avenue Rd.).

Tel: 416-961-1211

DISCOUNT INTERIOR DESIGN WAREHOUSE 🏠

This outlet carries just about everything for the home, including furniture and accessories, fabric and wall coverings. They have a fantastic garage sale the first Saturday after Labour Day with bargains of 80 % off retail pricing.

4155 Fairview St., Unit 16 (south of the Q.E.W. between Appleby Line and Walkers Line), Burlington.

Tel: 905 - 634-3439

Hours: M. to Thu. 10 - 5:30, F. 10 - 8, Sat. 10 - 5:30

home furnishings and appliances

ELTE CARPETS

80 Ronald Ave., (two blocks west of Dufferin Ave., north off Eglinton Ave.), Toronto.
Tel: 416-785-7885
Toll Free: 1-888-276-3583
Web site: www.elte.com
Hours: M to Sat 9-6, Thur. until 9; Sun. 12-5

EXCELLENCE IN ART WHOLESALE OUTLET

If you are looking for some new affordable art, (oil paintings) for your home, head to this location. Excellence in Art carries more than 4,000 original works and recreated masters as well as hundreds of Ready Made Frames for artwork and mirrors. Their on-site decorators will assist you in your selection, Prices range from $50 to $1500. Free home trials.

860 Denison Street, Unit 6 (east of Warden Ave. north of Steeles Ave.), Markham.
Tel: 905-305-0177
Website: www.excellenceinart.ca
Hours: Wed. 11 - 8; Sat. 12:30 - 4. or call for appointment

See advertisement on page A6

EXECUTIVE FURNITURE GARAGE SALE 🏠

If you are looking for some real bargains in furniture and accessories, get down to this sale with mega bargains of up to 90% off regular prices. They will be clearing out pre-rented and new bedroom, living room, dining room, office furniture and more at this blowout sale. While you are there, be sure to check out their cool classic car collection.

81 Tycos Drive (south of Lawrence Ave. off Dufferin St.) Toronto
Tel: 416-785-0932.
Hours: Call for sale date and hours

See advertisement on page A20

THE GRACIOUS LIVING CENTRE

160 West Beaver Creek Rd. (near Hwy. 7 & Leslie St.), Richmond Hill.
Tel: 905-731-4556
Hours: M. to F. 10 - 6, Sat. 10 - 5

---

home furnishings and appliances

G. H. JOHNSON'S

One of the best kept shopping secrets in Toronto. For years home, office and movie set designers, have prowled the 30,000 square feet of G H Johnson Trading. It is well worth a visit to this treasure trove of well-priced pieces suitable for any home.

   Location: 950 Dupont Street, Toronto
   Tel: 416-532-6700
   Hours: M. to Wed. 10-6, Thu. Fri. 10-9, Sat. 10-6, Sun. 12-5

See advertisement on page A10

HAUSER FURNITURE

   10815 Bathurst Street (Elgin Mills and Bathurst), Richmond Hill.
   Tel: 905-770-8742
   Hours: T.W. 10 -5; Thu.-F.. 12-8 Sat. 10 - 5; Sun. noon to 4.
   Call for other locations

HERITAGE CASTING AND IRONWORKS - FACTORY OUTLET

This manufacturer offers a wide selection of cast aluminum garden furniture, as well as lampposts, benches, planters, fountains and much more. It also offers a unique service of custom finishing, with a rainbow of colours, including antique finishes. By selling directly from its manufacturing facility, it is able to price their products competitively.

   1280 Fewster Dr., (Dixie Rd. & Eglinton Ave.), Mississauga.
   Tel: 905-238-2648
   Hours: M. to F. 8 - 4

Heroes - What a guy in a boat does.

A1

A2

A3

A4

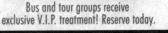

Establishing better sleep patterns since 1982.

Be it brand names like Wamsutta, Fieldcrest, Alexander Julian and Croscil, the finest Hutterite and Hungarian down bedding, or the choicest in iron furniture, nobody combines great prices with better products than Down Under. Come on over to any of 3 locations, there's a sale on every day.

Downtown	Mississauga	Markham
444, Yonge Street	5170 Dixie Road	5221 Hwy 7
College Park - Lower Level	South of Hwy 401	SW Corner- 7 & McCowan
(416) 598 2184	(905) 624 5854	(905) 305 9496
Free parking. Call for info		

We ship across Canada. Call toll free 1-800-36-DUVET or 1-888-624 6484.

www.downunder.on.ca

A8

A9

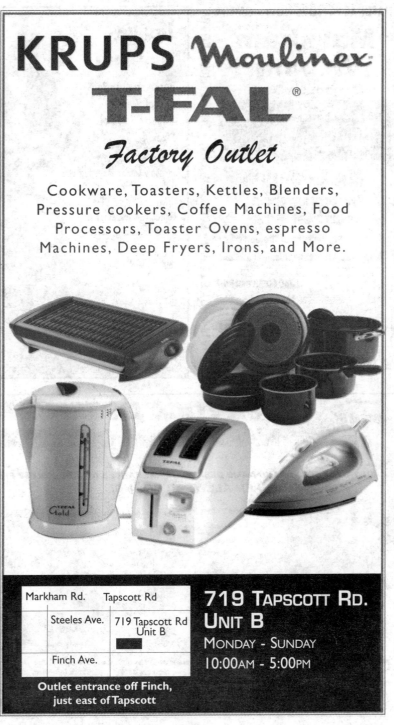
AII

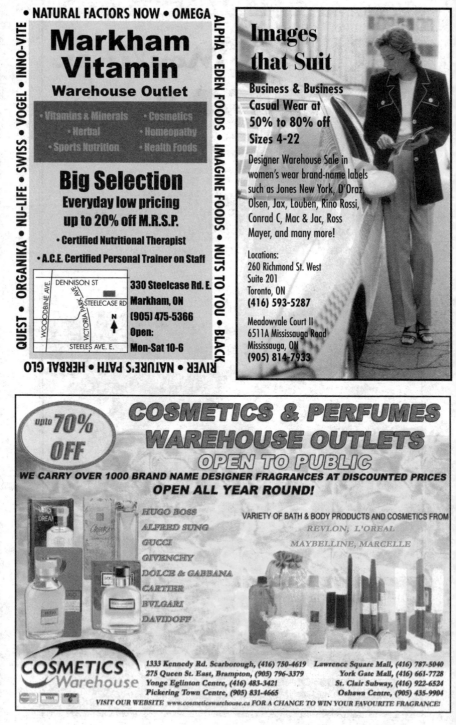
A12

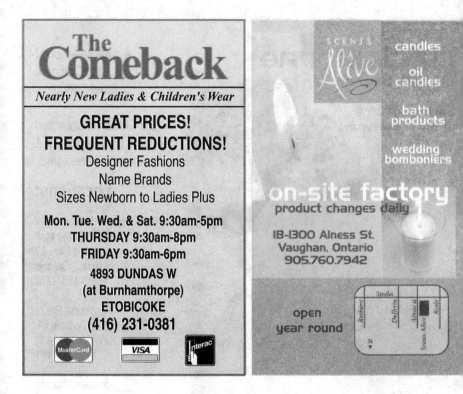

A14

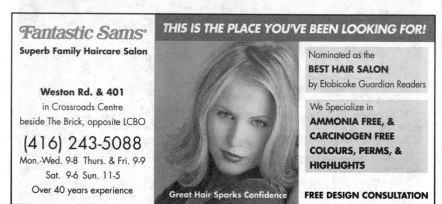

A17

A20

A21

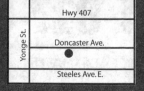

A24

A25

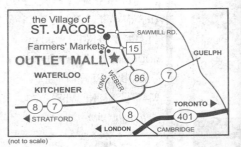

A29

A30

Notes

home furnishings and appliances

HERITAGE INTERIORS - 🛍️

A great time to buy fine quality furniture is at their semi-annual winter sale. The entire stock of upholstery, cabinets, mirrors and lamps are reduced up to 50%. Wonderful combinations of fabrics and upholstery can be found here and fabrics are up to 30% off now. Bring in your arm caps to make sure of a match as their occasional chairs are 60% off. No better time to pick up some great values for your home.

> 1100 Sheppard Ave. West (at the Allen Expressway), Toronto.
> Tel: 416-398-5560. Call for 2002-03 sale date.
> Hours: Monday to Wednesday 10 a.m. to 6 p.m., Thursday and Friday 10 a.m. to 8 p.m., and Saturday 10 am. to 6 p.m.

ALWAYS A GOOD SALE
Fine Traditional Furniture

Special dates: to follow

Jan - Feb	Store wide Sale
July	Birthday Sale
July - Aug	Store wide Sale
Dec 27	Boxing Day Sale

HERITAGE INTERIORS

1100 Sheppard at the Allen (416) 398-5560

IDOMO

> 1100 Sheppard Ave. West (at Allen Road, north of the 401, top of Spadina subway), Toronto.
> Tel: 416-630-3622
> Website: www.idomo.com
> Hours: M to F. 10-9, Sat. 10-6, Sun. 12-5

Bernadette - The act of torching a mortgage.

---

home furnishings and appliances

IKEA – ETOBICOKE
This new location is going to carry all 9,500 products in the IKEA range. You will find enticing specials on opening day such as Malko folding chairs for $9.95, tork laundry baskets $9.95 regularly $24.95, queen bed frames $99 regularly $199, assorted plants only $6.95 and much more. There are two level parking lots with 1,735 parking spaces and a highly interactive children's playland. Take a time-out for lunch in their largest restaurant in North America, complete with cappuccino bar, vegetarian offerings and special children's menu.

1475 The Queensway (west of Kipling Ave.), Etobicoke
Tel: 416-222-4532
Hours: M.-F. 10 a.m. to 9 p.m., Sat. 9 a.m. to 9 p.m., and
Sun. 10 a.m. to 6 p.m.

LEDA'S ATTIC FURNITURE OUTLET CENTRE
360 Clayson Rd. (north off Wilson Ave., just west of Hwy. #400), North York.
Tel: 416-745-9588
Hours: Call for sale dates and times.

LEISURELAND
Reconditioned air conditioners are sold here for half the price of a new one with the usual full warranty.

418 Consumers Rd., North York.
Tel: 416-492-2665
Hours: Hours are seasonal, please call for details.

MARBLE DEPOT
A builder friend, Bob, tipped us off to this outlet that has exceptional buys on slate, marble, granite and limestone. He emphasized that he really appreciates being able to browse and open skids to inspect the product before buying. They also carry 'feature strips' for that finishing touch, and inventory is always coming and going.

900 Caledonia Rd., (1 block south of Lawrence Ave.), Toronto.
Tel: 416-787-0391 or
Toll free: 1-888-379-1111
Hours: M. to F. 8 - 5:30, Sat. 8 - 5

home furnishings and appliances

MORETTE'S FURNITURE 🛋

For over 40 years, Morette's Furniture in Hillsburgh has been making traditional custom upholstered furniture. February is fabric sale month, with 20% off any fabric for new or re-upholstered furniture. There is a wide selection of styles and fabrics with a very knowledgeable staff available for your assistance. No charge for delivery in Toronto area.

15 Station St. (west on Hwy. 401 to Trafalgar Rd., go north 35 km. To Hillsburgh)
Tel: 905 846-2907 or 1-519 855-4905
Hours: Monday to Saturday 9:30 a.m. to 5:30 p.m,
Friday 9:30 a.m. to 9:30 p.m.

MOSSMAN'S APPLIANCE PARTS LTD. - PARTS DISTRIBUTOR

2273 Dundas St. W., Unit 12, Mississauga.
Tel: 905-569-8333
Hours: M. to F. 8 - 6, Sat. 9 – 3
Call for other locations.

MUSKOKA FURNITURE OUTLET

195 Wellington St. N., Unit 7 (Wellington Place Mall), Bracebridge.
Tel: 705-645-8183
Hours: Regular Hours: M. - Thu. & Sat. 9 - 6, F. 9 - 9
Summer Hours: M. to F. 9 - 9, Sat. 9 - 6, Sun. 12 – 4

MUSKOKA TEAK

We dropped in to this shop while recently in Muskoka, and were delighted with both the quality and price of the teak furnishings for sale. Two brothers own this business, and spend four months of each year in Indonesia sourcing the best quality they can find. And yes, they both speak the language fluently! A friend saw an identical item elsewhere for $200 less here – so promptly bought it! Of course good quality teak is never inexpensive, but we think you'll find great value here. A new container of items is arriving this month.

1005 Henshaw Lake Road, Unit 2A (just west of Port Carling), Muskoka
Tel: 705-765-1700. www.catsassimports.com
Hours: 7 days/week in the summer from 10 a.m. to 6 p.m.

POTTERY BARN

Lots of specials at the opening of their first Canadian outlet now open in the Eaton Centre. You'll find high end, casual home furnishings and decorative accessories that include bedding/bath, rugs, window treatments, lighting and more in a casual setting. We always loved browsing this store in the U.S., and it's great to have one of our own now!

220 Yonge Street – the Eaton Centre.

Tel: 416-597-0880

Hours: Monday to Friday 10:00 a.m. to 9:00 p.m., Saturday 9:30 a.m. to 7:00 p.m., Sunday noon to 6:00 p.m.

RAILSIDE ROAD GIFTWARE 📠

This sale, which has been running for 10 years offers a wide range of merchandise for gift giving & home accent, and of course, gifts for yourself! All merchandise is offered at wholesale or less including Seagull Pewter-handcrafted pewter from Nova Scotia, Umbra-world wide designer home accents, Solitudes nature sounds and music, Avalon instrumental music-holiday, big band, Celtic, Luna - handcrafted aluminum table ware, Among Friends-specialty collection of plush toys, Danica- linens,
Transversion-designer travel accessories, Plum Traders silver jewellery.
Other great gift items include candles, body care, frames, books, lighting, pillows and throws, drawer pulls, bathroom accessories, kitchen aprons and oven mitts. please call 416-441-9696 Ext 52 or see our ad in this guide.

WEBSITE: www.youngson.com\railsidselloff

132 Railside Rd. Don Mills.

Tel: 416 - 441-9696 for store hours and location directions.

See advertisement on page A26

Eyedropper - A clumsy ophthalmologist.

---

home furnishings and appliances

RIDPATH'S FINE FURNITURE WAREHOUSE SALE 🏠

197 Bartley Drive, Toronto (south of Eglinton off Bermondsey Ave)
Tel: 416-920-4444
Hours: Call for sale dates and times.

ROYAL FURNITURE WAREHOUSE

Thanks to a reader, we discovered this small Canadian owned operation that deals with 70-80 suppliers and has some great prices. They specialize in custom orders where you pick your furniture and then it can be made up with your preferred frames, stains and fabrics. Be sure to check out the bedroom suites on the second floor. No local delivery charges and they also set up all your furniture for you.

3560 Wolfedale Rd., (one block west of Mavis Rd., between
Burnhamthorpe Rd. and Dundas St.) Mississauga.
Tel: 905 848-4141.
Hours: Monday and Tuesday 9 a.m. to 6 p.m., closed Wednesday and Sunday, Thursday and Friday 9 a.m. to 9 p.m., Saturday 9 a.m. to 6 p.m.

SCOTT CLAY PRODUCTS

This is a great outlet to visit only a half hour from the Collingwood area. A Canadian manufacturer of quality flower pots, saucers, pedestals, sconces and lawn ornaments. Lots of different sizes of pots and planters, plus a cookware selection at this factory. Great buys on seconds, for half the original price. We picked up some fabulous planters for our gardens at bargain prices. Open 7 days a week.

278 Cook Street, Meaford, Ontario
Tel: 519-538-4769
Hours: Monday to Friday 8 a.m. to 5 p.m., Saturday and
Sunday 9 a.m. to 5 p.m.

Eclipse - What an English barber does for a living.

home furnishings and appliances

SEARS CANADA

We know people who shop here every week and get great bargains, so we decided to check them out. Their motto "Off Prices Everyday" translates to everyday low prices like furniture and appliances 10% to 30% off regular prices and 30% to 50% off the last Sears catalogue price on men's, women's and children's fashions. Check out the Saturday door crasher specials where you can get huge savings on specified items.

Rexdale Outlet, 2200 Islington Ave. N.
Tel: 416-401-4545
Don Mills Plaza, Markham, Pickering, Warden Woods, two in Dixie Outlet Mall and 2 in Brampton.
Call for your nearest location.
Hours: Monday to Friday 10 a.m. to 9 p.m., Saturday 9 a.m. to 6 p.m. and Sunday 11 a.m. to 5 p.m.

SESCOLITE - LIGHTING CLEARANCE CENTRE

4175 Fairview St., Burlington.
Tel: 905-632-8659
Hours: M. to W. 8:30 - 6, Thur. 8:30 - 9, F. 8:30 - 6, Sat. 9:30 - 6,
Sun. 12 - 4 (closed Sundays during Summer)

SHAW-PEZZO & ASSOCIATES INC. 🏷

20 Pine St. (2 lights west of Black Creek, south off Lawrence Ave.),
Toronto
Tel: 416-784-4400.
Hours: Monday to Friday 9 a.m. to 5 p.m., Saturday 10 a.m. to 5 p.m.

STEPTOE & WIFE ANTIQUES LTD. 🏷

322 Geary Ave. (one block north of Dupont St., west off Dufferin St.)
Toronto.
Tel: 416-780-1707 or
Toll free: 1-800-461-0060
Web Site: www.steptoewife.com
E-Mail: info@steptoewife.com
Hours: M. to F. 9 - 5

home furnishings and appliances

TERRACOTTA HOUSE AND SALTILLO IMPORTS

132 Railside Rd., Unit 8, (2 blocks east of Don Valley Parkway and south of Lawrence Ave.), Toronto.

Tel: 416-441-2224

Hours: M. to F. 9 - 6, Sat. 10 - 4

Call for other location and sale dates.

THE BACK DOOR SALE - 🏠

Here is another great sale to assist you in jump starting your Christmas shopping. There are lots of great bargains here on name brand collectibles, giftware, dolls, figurines, home décor, frames and Christmas décor. Even their wholesale prices have been reduced for this sale, with new product arriving daily.

25 Connell Ct., Unit 1, Etobicoke.

Tel: 416 –521-7299

Hours: Call for 2002 dates and hours.

THE ORIGINAL BRASS BED SHOPPES LTD. 🏠

119 Yorkville Ave. (2 blocks north of Bloor St. between Bay St. and Avenue Rd.), Toronto.

Tel: 416-968-6932

Call for sale dates and times.

THE URBAN MODE

389 Queen St. W., (east of Spadina Ave.), Toronto.

Tel: 416-591-8834

Hours: Hours change daily. Please call for hours.

Counterfeiters - Workers who put together kitchen cabinets.

---

home furnishings and appliances

TWO STAR DESIGN

Bruno has recently moved into larger premises which means he can carry even more of his creative stonework for your garden. Prices here are always competitive and include birdbaths, statues, benches, garden ornaments, planters and more. If you prefer the aged look in your garden, he will stain the items on request for an additional charge.

46 North Queen St., building 2 (North of The Queensway, west off Kipling Ave.), Etobicoke.

Tel: 416-231-7318

Hours: Monday to Friday 10:00 a.m. to 6:00 p.m., Saturday 9:00 a.m. to 4:00 p.m. Sunday by appointment.

VANI METAL ART - FACTORY OUTLET

6923 Steeles Ave. W., Units 56 & 57, (west of Hwy. 7, look for the wrought iron in the windows!), Etobicoke.

Tel: 416-213-0515

Hours: Call for hours.

Burglarize - What a crook sees with.

Control - A short, ugly inmate;

---

home decorating and housewares

ACADIA CANDLE OUTLET STORE
Carlisle Road and Hwy. 6,.(Take Hwy. 401 and exit at Hwy 6 - go south approximately 4 km.), Flamborough.
Tel: 905-777-9638
Hours: M to Fri 10- 6, Sat 9 – 6, Sun noon - 5

ALDERBROOK ANNUAL CHRISTMAS SALE 🎁
This sale will feature Christmas lights, decorations, trees and just about everything that this well known distributor carries - even a few Halloween items. Merchandise is end of lines, damaged packaging and samples.
5600 Finch Avenue East, (Finch Ave. and Tapscott Street), Scarborough.
Tel: 905-420-0494
Hours: Call for sale date and hours.

ANTHONY'S ART DESIGN LTD.
65 Densley Avenue, east off Keele Street, south of Lawrence.
Tel: 416-247-6113
Hours: M.-W. 10 - 3. (Closed in July)

ARCHAEOLOGY
160 Tycos Dr. Unit 1, (west off Dufferin St. north of Eglinton Ave.), Toronto
Tel: 416-787-6678
Hours: Call for sale dates and hours.

ARORA
This company operates a service location that offers great value on new and refurbished small electrical appliances and personal care products. All products come with a full warranty at prices that are 30 to 50% lower than retail.
488 Bloor St. W. (one block east of Bathurst Street), Toronto.
Tel: 416-532-8544
Hours: Monday to Friday 10 a.m. to 7 p.m., Saturday 10 a.m. to 6 p.m., Sunday noon to 5 p.m.

ARTEBRA GIFTS AND IMPORTS WAREHOUSE SALE - 🏠

An importer of houseware and giftware items from Italy, Brazil, Germany and the United States is having a showroom sale. Lots of good buys on unique, one-of-a-kind, glass pieces, espresso cups, dinnerware, vases and giftware at this small warehouse. We picked up very unique picture frames at very reasonable prices.

21 Royalcrest Road, Unit 2 (west off Martingrove Rd., north of Albion Rd.), Rexdale.
Tel: 416-747-1015
Hours: Call for 2002-03 sale dates. Monday to Friday noon to 8 p.m., Saturday and Sunday 10 a.m. to 5 p.m.

AURORA COLLECTIBLE FINE CHINA & CRYSTAL 🏠

Clearance of brand name crystal and china such as Waterford, Royal Doulton, Baccarat and Wallace & International Sterling Silver. Aurora also carries many pieces of hard-to-find, discontinued lines with savings up to 90% off. October and November Warehouse Sale.

1610 Midland Ave. (east of Kennedy Rd. and south of Lawrence Ave.), Scarborough.
Tel: 416-752-9300 or
Toll free: 1-800-668-3333
Hours: M., T. & Sat. 10 - 6, W. & F. 10 - 8, Sun. 12. - 5

AYUS OUTLET SALE 🏠

This importer of eclectic handicrafts is holding their first outlet sale. We found amazing items for the home that included beaded frames, incense burners, wonderful candles, fabric covered boxes and hand-carved wooden jewellery boxes. Our teenager thought this was the coolest sale ever, and I was also intrigued by the array of exotic items. Most items were under $10, and candles considerably less.

Sale will be held in the Scents Alive Factory Outlet Store at 1300 Alness Street (NW corner of Steeles Ave. and Alness St.), Toronto.
Tel: 905-760-7945
Hours: Call for date of 2003 sale. Monday to Saturday 10 a.m. to 5 p.m., Sunday noon to 5 p.m.

home decorating and housewares

BARNES & CASTLE

98 Orfus Rd. (off Dufferin St., south of Hwy. #401) Toronto.
Tel: 416-780-0226.
Hours: M.-F.- 10- 6, Sat. 10 -6

BARTOLINI 🏠

The plaster dust is always flying while this small manufacturer produces its wide range of items such as candle sticks, pedestals, planters and gargoyles. Shoppers will find excellent bargains on seconds and we invariably find something new in concrete or plaster to tuck in to the garden or home. Cash or cheques with ID. Call for warehouse sale dates and hours.

244 Brockport Dr., Unit 20, (first road west of hwy. 27, go north off Belfield Rd.) Etobicoke.
Hours: M. to F. 9-5:30

BATH N' BEDTIME 🏠 Semi Annual Warehouse Sale

These are the lowest prices of the year, so plan to stock up your linen closet now.   Choose from Fieldcrest, Springmaid, Wamsutta, Croscill, Martex, Dan River plus a whole lot more of bathroom and bedroom needs for home and cottages.   Large selection of duvet covers, sheets, towels, prints, mirrors, and home accent furniture. Four days only, everything is on for up to 75% off regular price.

502 Lawrence Ave. W. (Bathurst St. & Lawrence Ave.)
Tel: 416 781-8600, e-mail us at bathnbedtime@rogers.com
web site www.bathnbedtime.com.
Hours: Call for May and November sale dates. Thursday and Friday 9:30 a.m. to 9 p.m., Saturday 10 a.m. to 6 p.m., Sunday noon to 5 p.m.

See advertisement on page A2

BENIX AND CO. - WAREHOUSE OUTLET STORE 🏠

127 Cartwright Ave. (south of Hwy. 401, west off Dufferin St.), North York.
Tel: 416-784-0732
Hours: M. to F. 10 - 9, Sat. & Sun. 10 - 6

home decorating and housewares

BLACK & DECKER 🛒
The brand name of Black & Decker has earned the trust of power tool enthusiasts for generations. At their outlet store you'll find terrific deals year round on not only tools, but housewares and garden tools as well.

Warden Power Centre, 725 Warden Ave. (at St. Clair Ave.), Scarborough, ON.

Southworks Outlet Mall, 64 Grand Avenue, Cambridge, ON.

Cookstown Manufacturer's Outlet, Southeast corner Hwy. 400 & Hwy. 89.

Les Factoreries, St. Sauveur, Quebec.

See advertisement on page A4

BOMBAY COMPANY WAREHOUSE SALE 🛒
Save up to 60% off original showroom prices at this once a year, two day only sale. Choose from overstocks, discontinued or slightly damaged merchandise, which includes furniture, wall décor, home accessories and so much more. Bring your truck and packing materials to take away these terrific savings. Limited quantities available so be sure to arrive early for the best selection.

6100 Kenway Drive (Kennedy Rd. north of 401), Mississauga

Tel: 905 795-8800 (Call for sale date.)

Hours: Saturday 10 a.m. to 5 p.m., Sunday noon to 5 p.m.

See advertisement on page 101

C.W. & ASSOCIATES 🛒
6150 Dixie Rd., Units 2 and 3, (north of Hwy. 401, south of Courtney Park Dr., on the west Side), Mississauga.

Tel: 905-564-8521

Hours: Call for details.

CANADA STAINED GLASS SECONDS SALE 🛒
Once a year this manufacturer sells their slightly imperfect stained glass window hangings at up to 80% off retail. We saw a great selection that ranges from museum and historic reproductions on glass to birds and butterflies. Lovely for gift giving.

2775 Dundas Street West, Toronto

Tel: 416-763-6275 or 1-800-461-0590.

Hours: Call for sale date and hours.

home decorating and housewares

CAYNE'S SUPER HOUSEWARES

112 Doncaster Ave. (one traffic light north of Steeles Ave., east off Yonge St.), Thornhill.
Tel: 905-764-1188
Hours: M. to W. & Sat. 10 - 6, Thu. & F. 10 - 9, Sun. 11 - 5

CONCORD CANDLE CORP. - FACTORY OUTLET 🛍

This is a stop you will want to make. They have a large selection of firsts as well as seconds, including a large variety of prints, candle holders, garden accessories and many other items to choose from. While browsing the store don't forget to say "hi" to their candle makers and take some time to watch them carve candles. Each candle is hand dipped and hand carved so each one is unique in design and colour.

2315 Industrial Park Rd. (Innisfil Beach Road Exit off Hwy. 400, turn left on Industrial Park Rd.), Thornton.
Tel: 705- 431-7296
Hours: Seven days a week 9 - 5 Summer Hours M. – T. 9-5, Fri. 9-8, Sat. & Sun. 9-5

See advertisement on page A6

CORNING – OUTLET STORE

Cookstown Manufacturers Mall (Hwy. 400 & 89), Cookstown.
Tel: 705-458-9998
Call for other locations.

CONSOLIDATED BOTTLE COMPANY

77 Union Street (one block northwest of Old Weston Road and St. Clair Ave. W.), Toronto.
Tel: 416-656-7777
Hours: M.-F. 8:30-4; Closed weekends.

COUNTRY FLOORS

321 Davenport Road, Toronto.
Tel: 416-922-9214
Hours: M. to F. 9 - 5

home decorating and housewares

DANSK WAREHOUSE SALE 🏠

Save on fabulous new selections of kitchenware, tableware, cookware, holiday accessories, décor and table linens. Perfect time to stock up on items for weddings, showers, birthdays and hostess gifts. There is something for everyone on your list here and many items are up to 75% off regular prices. Shelves are restocked daily.

Wheelchair accessible. May/June and Nov./Dec.&.Warehouse Sales.

690 Horner Ave. (take Kipling exit south of Q.E.W. to Evans Ave., east to Horner Ave.), Toronto.

Tel: 416-259-1127. Call for sale dates.

Hours: Mon. to Fri. 10 a.m. to 8 p.m., Sat. 10 a.m. to 5 p.m., Sun. 11 a.m. to 5

See advertisement on page A2

DESIGNERS WALK SUMMER SALE 🏠

Ground Floor Garage, 160 Pears Avenue, sidewalks and roads (north of Davenport Rd. west off Avenue Rd), Toronto.

Tel: 416-961-1211

Call for 2002-3 sale dates and hours.

DISCOUNT INTERIOR DESIGN WAREHOUSE 🏠

Good taste doesn't need to be expensive - just drop into this shop and you'll discover this annual sale featuring 20 - 80% savings on hundreds of items that include furniture, lamps, pictures and accessories.

4155 Fairview Street (QEW east to Burlington, exit at Appleby Line. Go south, and right at Fairview Street), Burlington.

Tel: 905-634-3439

Hours: M. to W. 10:00 - 5:30, T. to F. 10:00 - 9:00 Sat. 10:00 - 5:30 Sun. noon - 5:00.

If a turtle doesn't have a shell, is he homeless or naked?

EAST PORT MFG. 🗄

Planning on doing some spring decorating? This two-day sale then is a must for you. Wonderful placemats, chair pads, throw cushions and tablecloths, plus drapery toppers and decorative wood poles for drapery can be found here. Lots of beautiful fabrics available and they will take orders for you to have made up. Be sure to bring your window and table measurements with you. Everything is well priced below wholesale. Cash and Visa only and all sales are final.

1151 Gorham Street, Units 5 & 6 (one street south of Davis Dr. off Leslie St.) Newmarket.

Tel: 905 830-0816

Hours: Call for sale date and hours.

EBC GIFTS & COLLECTIBLES WAREHOUSE SALE 🗄

There are values up to 70% off retail at this warehouse sale. Choose from their large selection of well known brand name crystal imported from Europe, lamps, vases, stemware, bowls, ice buckets, candlesticks, trays, baskets, brand name flatware, pots and pans and more. Merchandise is first quality and perfect for gift giving. All sales are final, cash and Visa only.

35 East Beaver Creek Rd., Unit 1A (rear) (north of Hwy. #7, and east of Leslie St.) Richmond Hill.

Tel: 905-764-0795.

Hours: Call for sale dates and hours.

EGLINTON WHOLESALE PAINT & HARDWARE

536 Eglinton Ave. W. (2 blocks W. of Avenue Rd.), Toronto.

Tel: 416-485-2352

Hours: M. to F. 9:30 – 5:30, Sat. 9:30 – 5:00

ERIN-ROTHWELL

60 Main St., (north on Hwy. #10 to Hwy. #24 or Charleston Side Rd., then west to Erin).

Toll free: 1 800-274-8726

Hours: T-F. 10-6. Sat. 10 –6 Sun. 11 - 5.

home decorating and housewares

EUROPEAN HOTEL & RESTAURANT IMPORTS LTD.
This commercial kitchenware supplier is open to the public year-round, offering excellent quality and wholesale prices on flatware, china, glassware and commercial-grade kitchenware.

343 Horner Ave. (off Kipling Ave., three blocks south of Evans Ave.), Etobicoke.

Tel: 416-253-9449

Hours: M. to F. 8:30 - 5, call for weekend hours

EXCELLENCE IN ART
If you are looking for some new art for your home and are unable to afford an original Monet or Matisse, make sure you head out to this location. They carry over 4,000 oil paintings, hundreds of unique ready-made ornate and contemporary frames for artwork and mirrors. They have decorators on site to assist you in your selection and prices range from only $50 to $1500. Free home trials.

860 Denison Street, Unit 6, (east of Warden Ave. north of Steeles Ave.), Markham.

Tel: 905 - 305-0177

Hours: Wed. 10:30 a.m. to 8 p.m. and Sat. 12:30 p.m. to 4 p.m..

Other hours, call for appointment 9 a.m. to 5 p.m. Mon. to Sat.

See advertisement on page A6

GIANT XMAS WAREHOUSE SALE –
Rock bottom prices at this warehouse sale. One of Canada's largest importers of home décor items has for the first time, opened their doors for a tremendous holiday clearance sale. We found great items such as wooden benches at $169 regular $299, kitchen trolleys from $50, wicker cabinets and tables, and colourful magazine racks at $5. Be sure and check out their scratch and bent room where the bargains get even better!

Supertest Rd. Unit 12 (left off Dufferin St. north of Finch Ave.) North York.

Tel: 416-736-0094

Hours: Call for hours and sale date.

---

home decorating and housewares

GIFTS THAT MAKE A DIFFERENCE 📦

This non-profit organization carries handmade crafts, including Xmas decorations, wooden mobiles, wrought iron candelabras and hand-painted ceramics, all from craft co-ops in Southeast Asia. No cheques. T.B.A. Warehouse Sale.

388 Carlaw Ave., Unit W-11, (at Dundas St. E.), Toronto.
Tel: 416-720-2223

GIFT IDEAZ 📦

Gift Ideaz located in the Richview Plaza is a unique store with a heart. Specializing in personal gifts and home décor/accessories, Gift Ideaz will welcome you with a smile, serve Free Espresso coffee while you shop and gift wrap your purchases in one of several quality papers before you leave. On top of all that, they donate a percentage of their annual sales to breast cancer research including 25% of all sales on September 29th.

Location: Richview Plaza, 250 Wincott Drive, Etobicoke.
Tel: 416-248-4403
Hours: M. to Wed. 10-7; Thu. Fri. 10-8; Sat. 9:30-6
Sun. 11-5. (Closed Sundays during July and August)
Website: www.giftideaz.com

Inspire your imagination, *unwrap* your dreams.

GiftIdeaz is dedicated to bringing you unique and wondrous gifts from Canada and around the world.

Gift Ideaz

Visit our website **www.giftideaz.com** or our store at Richview Square, On Eglinton just east of Kipling, **416.248.4403**

Mon.-Wed. 10-7, Thurs.-Fri. 10-8, Sat. 9:30-6, Sun. 11-5

GOODMAN'S CHINA

1136 Centre Street, Thornhill.
Toll free: 1-800-665-8187
Hours: M. T. & Sat. 9:30 - 6, W. & Thu. 9:30 - 8, Sun. 12 - 5

GRAND REGAL INTERNATIONAL LTD. - WAREHOUSE SALE 📦

1255A Unit 2, Reid St., Richmond Hill.
Tel: 905-886-6817

home decorating and housewares

HOME & GARDEN DECORATORS WAREHOUSE SALE 🏠
70 Wingold Avenue (west off Dufferin St., south of Lawrence Ave.), Toronto.
Tel: 416-783-0230
Call for sale dates and times.

HOMESENSE
Brampton, Woodbridge, Ancaster, London, Kingston, Ottawa (Call for hours and location nearest you).
Toll free: 1-866-HOME-707

IDEAL PAINTS – FACTORY OUTLET
The "IDEAL" paint store! Not only do they sell their locally manufactured 100% Acrylic paints and stains, they also distribute many premium products such as Cabot, Sikkens and Minwax stains. The factory outlet also carries a large variety of painting accessories to help out the least experienced to the most experienced painter/hobbyist, all at wholesale prices.
172 Belfield Rd. (east of Hwy. 27), Rexdale/Etobicoke.
Tel: 416-243-7578
Hours: M. to F. 7 - 5:30

The Shoestring Shopping Guide relys on you our readers to refer your favourite shopping experiences and locations. Please email your finds to Cathie Mostowyk at shoestringshopping@rogers.com or Linda Sherman at lsherman@idirect.ca

JOBSON AND SONS LTD. 🗄

Lots of great home decor items in this sale including bedding, comforters, duvet covers, cushions, lampshades, fabric, trims and more. Stock consists of end-of-lines, seconds and overstocks, and is priced at least 50% off. Bring in an old lamp that needs a new shade and match it up for size and colour. April, May, June, October, November & December are possible months for warehouse sales. E-mail us to be placed on sale notice list; sales@jobsonandsons.com.

5925 Tomken Road, Unit 9 (north of Hwy. 401, corner of Britannia Road), Mississauga.
Tel: 905-795-1019
Website: www.jobsonandsons.com/warehousesale
Hours: TBA

JULMAR IMPORTS

Wonderful items abound from this manufacturer and designer at wholesale prices.
You'll find beautiful hand made pottery, black earthenware, charger plates, white ceramic jugs, teapots, rice bowls, place mats and huge flowerpots. We also picked up some Christmas decorations to start us off for the upcoming season.

153 Bridgeland Ave, Unit #7 (south of Hwy. 401, west off Dufferin St.) Toronto
Tel: 416 782-8332.
Hours: Call for sale dates and hours.

KARCHER WAREHOUSE SALE 🗄

6975 Creditview Rd., Unit 2 Mississauga
Tel: 905-672-8233
Call for sale date and hours.

KITCHEN STUFF PLUS SUPERWAREHOUSE

Where else can you fill up a shopping bag full of great stuff for your home for under $25.00? You will find real savings up to 60% off everyday, throughout the store.
They carry name brands such as Umbra, Henckels, Lagostina, Cuisinart and Proctor Silex. This week check out steel step cans in a range of sizes from as low as $15, aromatherapy candle jars for just $5 and a Henckels parer/peeler

set for only $6.

You won't be leaving this outlet empty handed!

> 76 Orfus Rd. (south of Hwy. #401, off Dufferin St.) Toronto.
> Tel: 416-907-5195. Call for other locations.
> Hours: Monday to Wednesday 10 a.m. to 6 p.m., Thursday and Friday
> 10 a.m. to 9 p.m., Saturday 9:30 a.m. to 6 p.m., and Sunday 11 a.m. to
> 6 p.m.

MADAWASKA DOORS INC.

> King Twp. R.R. #3, Schomberg.
> Tel: 905-859-4622 or Toll free: 1-800-483-2358
> Website: www.madawaska-doors.com
> Call for appointment.

MCINTOSH & WATTS - WAREHOUSE OUTLETS

> Off the 401 Hwy. south of the border with Quebec, Lancaster.
> Tel: 613- 347-2461
> Hours: M. to Sat. 9:30 - 6, Sun. & holidays 11 – 5

MIKASA (CANADA) INC. 🏠

> 161 McPherson Street (west of Warden Avenue, north of Steeles),
> Markham.
> Tel: 905 - 474-0880
> Call for sale dates and hours.

**Rectitude (n.), the formal, dignified demeanor assumed by a
proctologist immediately before he examines you.**

---

home decorating and housewares

MIRAGE 🏠
746 Warden Avenue, Unit 3 (South of Eglinton Avenue, north of St. Clair Avenue), Scarborough.
Tel: 416-285-7991
Hours: 9:00 a.m. - 5:00 p.m.

MONARCH PAINTS LIMITED
3620 Dufferin St. (Dufferin St. and Wilson Ave., just north of Hwy. 401), North York.
Tel: 416-635-6560
Hours: M. to W. 7 - 6, Thu. & F. 7 - 7, Sat. 8 - 5

MOUNT 'N SEAL
10 Brentcliffe Rd. (south of Eglinton Ave.), Leaside.
Tel: 416-423-9975
Hours: M. to F. 9 - 5, Sat. 11 – 2, Summer Hours: M. to F. 9 - 5

NABOR'S PAINTS
In the mood for decorating? We found a great place to help you out.
They have a colour preview system where they will make up a sample quart of flat latex paint, your choice of colour for $5. Take it home and paint a small area on your wall. You evaluate the colour, and when you return it, you get $2.50 off every gallon of that colour you purchase of Benjamin Moore or Para paint. The Kingston Rd. store also has colour visualization software that scans the photo of your home and can change the colour that you pick to see if it would be suitable. An excellent way not to make a costly error.
2184 Queen St. E., (west of Beech Ave.), Toronto
Tel: 416-690-7596
Hours: M.-F. 8 a.m. to 6 p.m., Sat. 9 a.m. to 6 p.m. and Sun. 9 a.m. to 5 p.m.
2261 Kingston Rd., (west of Midland Ave. in Ridgemoor Plaza), Scarborough.
Tel: 416-274-3855.
M.-F. 9 a.m. to 6 p.m., Sat. 9 a.m. to 5 p.m

NEO-IMAGE CANDELIGHT LTD.

Nothing evokes the Christmas spirit more than soft candlelight, especially scented ones that fill the home with warmth and Yuletide scents. This outlet carries a wide variety of candles, votives, mini jars and gift sets at prices that are tough to beat - their small scented mini jars are only $1.75. Open year round, but especially nice at Christmas.

1331 Blundell Road, (south of Dundas Street, west of Dixie Road), Mississauga.
Tel: 905 - 273-3682
Hours: Monday to Saturday 10 a.m. to 4 p.m.

ONTARIO PAINT AND WALLPAPER

275 Queen Street East, (east of Sherbourne St.), Toronto.
Tel: 416-362-5127
Hours: M. to F. 7 - 6, Sat. 8:30 - 5:30

ONEIDA FACTORY OUTLET

8699 Stanley Ave. S. (take the Q.E.W. west to McLeod Rd., go south and turn right on to Stanley Ave.), Niagara Falls.
Tel: 905-356-9691
Hours: M. to Sun. 9:30 - 5

OLD COLONY CANDLE FACTORY OUTLET

66 Line 15 South, RR #1 (Oro-Medonte, Line 15 off Hwy. 11), Orillia.
Tel: 705- 325-0349
Hours: Open 7 days a week 10-5; Summer hours: M. – T. 10-5; Fri. 10-8, Sat. & Sun. 10-5

PAINT, WALLPAPER AND FABRIC SOURCE

85 Doncaster Ave. (North of Steeles Ave., east off Yonge St.), Thornhill.
Tel: 905-881-8828
Hours: M. - F. 7 - 6, Sat. 9:30 - 5

PADERNO FACTORY STORE

Cookstown Manufacturers Mall, (building B) Hwy 400 and 89, Cookstown.
Tel: 705-458-2197
Hours: M. to Sat. 9 - 5, Sun. 12 - 4
Call for other locations.

PERFECT FLAME CANDLE COMPANY

You'll enjoy this small outlet, which offers unique hand poured candles, scented votive pillars, tapers and selected giftware at outlet prices. They'll also do special candles for weddings and other events, as well as offering a wide selection of candle making supplies.

1616 Matheson Blvd. E., units 25 and 26 (north of Eglinton Ave.), Mississauga.
Tel: 905-625-2521
Hours: M.-F. 9-6, Sat. 10 - 6

PIONEER STAR (CANADA) LTD.

55 West Beaver Creek, Unit 8, (Leslie St. & Hwy. 7 area), Richmond Hill.
Tel: 905-709-0909

PLAITER PLACE

In the heart of Chinatown, this small unassuming store sells bamboo mats from $2.00, small wicker furnishing, blinds of paper and bamboo, place mats, lampshades, baskets and much more. They are literally stuffed to the ceiling with inventory at very reasonable prices and good quality.

384 Spadina Avenue (College St. & Dundas St.) Toronto.
Tel: 416 593-9734
Hours: Monday to Saturday 11:30 to 7 p.m., Sunday 1 p.m. to 6 p.m

PRECIDIO WAREHOUSE SALE

Just in time for pool and patio season! This sale offers an amazing variety of acrylic barware, tumblers, pitcher and tray sets as well as matching melamine dinnerware. Prices are great, and there's no better time to stock up either for yourself or for gift giving.

35 Precidio Court (north of Hwy. 7, west of Airport Road), Brampton
Tel: 905-790-0790 or 1-800-387-2304
Hours: Call for sale dates and hours.

home decorating and housewares

PREMIER CANDLE CORP.
760 Britannia Rd., Mississauga.
Tel: 905-795-8833
Hours: M. to F. 9-5, Sat. 9-12, and for holiday season only, Sun. 10-5

PICTURE PICTURE
A heaven for anyone looking for a variety of latest prints and designs for home décor. They offer framed art, mirrors, custom framing, plaque mounting and canvas transfer. Their prices are guaranteed to be the lowest and for summer there's an additional 25% off on all imported framed mirrors.
122 Cartwright Ave. (south of Hwy. 401, off Dufferin St.), Toronto.
Tel: 416-787-9827
Hours: M- F - 10 – 6, Sat- 10 - 6 Sun.- noon to 5

See advertisement on page A18

POSTERS INTERNATIONAL
Locations:New showroom is at 1200 Castlefield Ave., (north side, west of Dufferin St.), Toronto,
Tel: 416-789-7156.
Hours: M. to F. 9-5

PRETTY RIVER GENERAL STORE
Hwy 124, 4 km. South of Collingwood, Village of Nottawa.
Tel: 705-444-6923
Hours: M.-Sat. 10-6, Sun. 11 -5.

ROB McINTOSH CHINA & CRYSTAL SHOPS
WAREHOUSE SALE
Superstore located at the northeast corner of Hwy. 7 and Weston Rd., Woodbridge.
Tel: 905-264- 3533.
For other locations, check their website at
www.robmcintoshchina.com/home.ithml.

ROYAL DOULTON - WAREHOUSE SALE 📠
Metro East Trade Centre, 1899 Brock Rd. (northeast corner of Hwy. 401 and Brock Rd.), Pickering.
Tel: 905-427-0744
Call for sale dates, hours and location.

RICH HILL CANDLES AND GIFTS - FACTORY OUTLET

One of Muskoka's must unique family attractions-truly a destination well worth the drive for a terrific selection of gifts, treasures, curiosities and candles. See candles being hand crafted. Create your own candles in the factory crafting room. Shop for a tremendous selection of candle styles, fragrances and colours, all offered at the best factory outlet prices.

9 Robert Dollar Dr. (Just off Hwy. #118), Bracebridge.

Tel: 705-645-3068

Hours: M. to Sat. 9 - 5, open Sun.in the summer and on long weekends 10 – 4.

SAMUEL HARRIS (1994) LTD.

Great prices at this find if you are looking to update your boat or family vehicle. They carry a wide selection of auto trims, vinyl upholsteries, vinyl wallcovering, foams, seat belting and carpeting and the prices are unbeatable. Pick up material here also to make your own BBQ covers and table toppers.

7131 Edwards Blvd. Unit #2, (Derry Rd. and Hwy. #10), Mississauga.

Tel: 905-795-9795

Hours: M- F 7:30 - 4:30, Sat 8 - noon

SCENTS ALIVE'S REAL FACTORY OUTLET SALE 🝠

Candles, body care, gifts, accessories and so much more. This is where the gift stores come to find bargains and now you can too. A step back to when a factory outlet was actually at the factory. Everyday new merchandise is brought out from excess production in the factory and sold at 50% - 85% off. There is always something new and exciting. A beautiful showroom full of wonderful smells from the factory. Easy to get to and lots of free parking. Open 7 days with frequent featured goods sales.

1300 Alness St., (North West corner of Alness and Steeles. East of York University),Vaughan. .

Call for hours and directions; 905 - 760-7942.

email; outlet@vegewax.com. website; www.scentsalive.com

See advertisement on page A14

home decorating and housewares

SWISS PEAK OUTLET SALE ⬛

Lots of gift ideas here where they are selling the finest in overstocked and discontinued European brand products. It is small, but they have lots of copper and stainless steel cookware, Peugeot pepper mills, wine accessories, Wenger Swiss army and household knives, Swiss Military watches, raclettes, fondues and lots of kitchen gadgets at outlet prices.

    35 East Beaver Creek Rd. Unit 3, (north of Hwy. #7, east of Leslie St.) Richmond Hill.

    Tel: 905-764-6068.

    Hours: Call for sale date and times.

SUPER ELECTRIC CO. ⬛

Great prices on a variety of overstocked, discontinued and refurbished items abound at this sale. Look for humidifiers, heaters, hair dryers, water coolers, ceiling fans and lots more at prices up to 70% off.

    Location: 500 Esna Park Dr. (one block north of Steeles Ave. E), Markham.

    Hours: Monday - Friday 8 a.m. - 4:30 p.m.

    Tel: 905 - 415-1700

T-FAL FACTORY OUTLET

A wonderful little outlet if you are looking for electrical appliances or cookware, Toasters, Kettles, Blenders, Pressure Cookers, Coffee Machines, Food Processors, Toaster Ovens, Espresso Machines, Deep Fryers, Irons and more - usually at discounts that range between 15 and 50%. All items are either discontinued or refurbished, which means there may be a packaging defect or a small scratch. Brand names include: T-Fal, Krups and Moulinex

    719 Tapscott Avenue, Unit B (east of Markham Road, between Steeles Ave. and Finch Ave.), Scarborough. Outlet entrance off Finch, near Tapscott.

    Tel: 416-299-8541

    Hours: Mon. to Sun. 10 to 5   See advertisement on page A11

TEN THOUSAND VILLAGES - IMPORTER'S STORE

This is a volunteer-operated, non-profit Mennonite warehouse and store that imports and sells thousands of neat & unique items from 35 developing nations. Their Thrift Shop located in the same building is one of the nicest that we have seen. The shop has several quilts for sale as well as clothes and housewares.

> 65 Heritage Drive (south off Hwy. 7/8 at the Beams/Hamilton Rd. stoplight), New Hamburg.
> Tel: 519-662-1879
> Hours: M. to F. 9 - 5, Sat. 10 - 4
> 2599 Yonge St., Toronto.
> Tel: 416-932-1673
> M. to F. 9-5, Sat. 10-4
> Stores also in Waterloo, Stratford and Niagara-on-the-Lake.

TERRACE GALLERY AND ART & FRAME

If 'cabin fever' is affecting your point of view may we suggest some new art work to brighten your four walls? Excellent discounts are offered on thousands of framed pieces with images from every category, from signed prints by Group of Seven artists, to sports, Impressionists, country and farm style, classical etc. etc.

> Terrace Gallery Showroom 50 Esna Park Dr., (4 lights north of Steeles Ave. and east off Woodbine Ave.), Markham. VISA, Mastercard, Interac and cheques with ID accepted;
> Art & Frame 125 Ashwarren Dr., (east off Keele St., between Finch and Sheppard Ave.), Downsview VISA, Interac, cheques with ID.
> Hours: Call for hours

THE COLLECTOR'S CUPBOARD

> 20 Freel Lane, Unit #6 (behind the train station), Stouffville.
> Tel: 905-640-9810
> Tue.-F. 9:30-5
> Closed Sun. and Mon.

THE DOOR FACTORY

> 114 Kennedy Rd. S. Brampton.
> Tel: 905-796-3373
> Hours: M, T. and Fri 9-6, W. and Thu. 9-8 and Sat 9-3.

THE FERN GROUP WAREHOUSE SALE 🗃

Everyone loves decorating with candles at this time of year, so there's no better time to drop into this manufacturer of candles and potpourri. Ends of lines, and discontinued designs and colours will be cleared at 25%-50% off retail, and they'll pay GST and PST. We loved their vanilla candles in a jar, as well as the festive colours of their pillar candles. You'll also find a selection of Christmas paper tableware.

> 175 Fenmar Dr. (two lights north of Finch Ave., west off Weston Rd.), North York.
> Tel: 416-749-0480
> Hours: Call for sale date and times, cash or Visa only.

THE FINNISH PLACE 🗃

You will feel like you're in Finland as you walk into this small store. Unique items that include tableware in Arabia patterns will be on sale at 30 to 50% off. Lovely quality and thirty years of design experience create a warm ambience for this shopping excursion.

> 5463 Yonge St. (three blocks south of Finch Ave.), Toronto
> Tel: 416-222-7575
> Hours: Call for sale dates. Monday to Friday 10 a.m. to 6 p.m., (until 7 on Thursday and Friday), Saturday 10 a.m. to 5 p.m., closed Sunday.

THE GARDEN ROOM

> 1672 Kingston Road, (just east of Birchcliff Ave.), Scarborough.
> Tel: 416-690-6987
> Hours: M.-Sat. 10-6, Sun.- noon to 5.

THE GOLD LEAF COMPANY

> 17 Ruggles Avenue, Unit #6 (east off Langstaff Road south of Hwy #7), Thornhill .
> Tel: 905-731-3909
> Call for sale dates and hours.

home decorating and housewares

THE UMBRA FACTORY SALE 🏠

Umbra is well known for high quality designer items that include fabulous frames, drapery hardware, clocks, and other accessory items. Prices at this sale are always excellent, so drop in and you just may be able to finish up your shopping in one spot! December Warehouse Sale.

Tel: 416-299-0088

Call for 2002 sale location and dates. 1-800-387-5122

THE VICTORIAN SHOPPE

334 Kingston Rd. (north side, east of Woodbine Ave.), Scarborough.

Tel: 416-698-5547

Hours: T., Thu. to Fri. 11 - 7, Sat. and Sun.11-6

THE WEATHERVANE 🏠

Each year this quaint country store gears up for their annual Christmas Anniversary Sale. Everything, including new Christmas stock is on sale. Try a scratch and save with everything purchased up to 25% off. A good excuse for a little country outing and pick up home accents, gourmet delights, Christmas decorations, candles and much more.

18424 Hurontario St. (Hwy #10, one block north of Regional Road #24, Caledon Village.

Tel: 519 – 927-9773

Hours and Dates: Call for details.

UPPER CANADA SOAP & CANDLE MAKERS - FACTORY OUTLET

Over 3,000 sq. ft. jammed with first quality bath and body care items, soaps and fragrant mist for the body and pillow; bubble bath crystals and oils as well as massage creams to pamper yourself. Candles and accessories to decorate your home and enhance your dinner table at 50% off retail. Treat yourself to new sheets, comforters and shams at greatly reduced prices. You'll also see table linens, bath towels and shower accessories at 40% to 50% off retail. Just for Christmas gift giving name brand children's wear such as Peter Rabbit, Pooh and Oshkosh will be arriving, all reduced by 50%.

1510 Caterpillar Rd. (N.E. corner of Dixie Rd. and The Queensway), Mississauga.

Tel: 905-897-1710

Hours: M-F 10-5, Sat. 10-4, Sun. closed

VENATOR ELECTRONICS - CLEARANCE CENTRE

55 East Beaver Creek, (northwest of either Leslie St. or Hwy. 7),
Richmond Hill.
Tel: 905-602-8400
Hours: M. to W. 9 - 6, Thu. & F. 9 - 8, Sat. 9 - 5

VENDABLES GIFT WAREHOUSE OUTLET

Treasures are to be found here, at greatly reduced prices, on some discontinued lines, seconds and samples of brand names such as Fitz & Floyd, Kosta
Boda, Royal Worcester and more. Gift ideas galore for the kitchen, garden and
all the Martha Stewarts on your list.

55 East Beaver Creek Rd. (north of Hwy. #7 and Leslie St.), Richmond
Hill.
Tel: 905-731-3187.
Hours: Tue.-Fri. 10 a.m. to 8 p.m., Sat. 10 a.m. to 5 p.m.,
Sun. noon to 5 p.m

VARIMPO-CANHOME- WAREHOUSE SALE 🏠

5320 Timberlea Blvd. (west of Tomken Road and south of Matheson
Road), Mississauga.
Tel: 905-624-6262
Hours: Call for hours

WILLIAM ASHLEY WAREHOUSE SALE 🏠

Some of us wait all year for this one! You'll find great selections on name
brand dinner sets, crystal, stainless and silver flatware, silver serving pieces,
vases, bowls, barware, house wares, gourmet cookware, executive gifts, children's gifts, a Christmas Shop and much more at savings up to 90%. There are
40,000 sq. ft. of incredible savings, so put on your shopping shoes and have fun
at this once-a-year sale! October 30th. – November 24th. 2002.

62 Railside Rd. (south of Lawrence Ave. between Don Valley Parkway and
Victoria Park) Toronto.
Tel: 416-515-SALE.
Hours: Wed., Thur. Fri. 10-9; Sat-Sun. 10-6, Mon-Tues. closed.

See advertisement on inside back cover

home decorating and housewares

WORLD OF GIFTS AND HOME DÉCOR

Lots of great gift giving ideas which include fountains, wall plaques, clay planters, vases and even unique fogging bowls (we didn't know what they were either. They set the mood for relaxation)! Prices are very competitive.

6725 Pacific Circle (south of Derry Rd.), Mississauga.
Tel: 905-670-3490
Hours: Call for 2002-3 sale dates. Monday to Friday 9:00 a.m. to 4:30 p.m., Saturday 10:00 a.m. to 2:00 p.m.

More Bible revisions by minors
Actual responses to bible questions on a test given to elementary school kids.

•Lot's wife was a pillar of salt by day, but a ball of fire by night.

•The Jews were a proud people! and throughout history they had trouble with the unsympathetic Genitals.

•Samson slayed the Philistines with the axe of the Apostles.

•Moses led the Hebrews to the Red Sea, where they made unleavened bread which is bread without any ingredients.

•The Egyptians were all drowned in the dessert. Afterwards, Moses went up on Mount Cyanide to get the ten ammendments.

•The first commandment was when Eve told Adam to eat the apple.

---

fabric and linen

AU LIT OUTLET
   598 Mt. Pleasant Road (three blocks south of Eglinton Ave. E.), Toronto.
   Tel: 416-489-5245.
   Hours: M.-F. 10-6, Sat. 10-5, Sunday noon to 5.

BATH N' BEDTIME
Save up to 75% at this semi-annual warehouse sale where the white sale never
ends. Lots of selection that includes Fieldcrest, Springmaid, Cannon,
Wamsutta, Croscil, Martex and much more. A great time to stock up on your
bathroom and bedroom needs as these prices are their lowest of the year.
Four locations, great pricing year round.
   502 Lawrence Ave. West (Bathurst & Lawrence), Toronto.
   Tel: 416-781-8600
   1755 Pickering Parkway (401 & Brock Road), Pickering.
   Tel: 905-428-0007
   765 Exeter Road (Exeter & Wellington St.), London.
   Tel: 519-686-1759
   410 Lewis Road (QEW and
   Fruitland Road), Stoney Creek.
   Tel: 905-643-2114
   Hours: Call for sale dates and hours.
                                                    See advertisement on page A2

CAMBRIDGE TOWEL & BEDDING MILL OUTLET-
Factory Outlet Store
The Cambridge Mill Outlet is an exciting textile store filled with a complete
array of Canadian terry bath products as well as bedding and kitchen textiles.
   South Works Outlet Mall, 64 Grand Avenue S., Cambridge.
   Hours: M. to W. 9:30 – 6, Thu. & F 9:30 – 9, Sat. 9 – 6, Sun. 11 - 5
   341 Ottawa St. N., Hamilton.
   Hours: M. to Thu. & Sat. 9 - 5: F. 9 - 9, Sun. 12 - 4
   Cookstown Mfrs. Outlet Mall, (400 & 89 Hwy.) Cookstown.
   Hours: M. to F. 10 – 9, Sat. and Sun. 9-6.
   Canada One Factory Outlet, 7500 Lundy's Lane, Niagara Falls.
   Hours: M.-F. 10-9, Sat. and Sun. 10-6.
   St. Jacobs Mall 25 Benjamin Rd., Waterloo.
   Hours: M.-F. 9:30-9, Sat. 8:30-6, Sun. noon-6

---

fabric and linen

CANADA STAINED GLASS SECONDS SALE –

Once a year these slightly imperfect window hangings are sold at up to 80% off retail. Lovely to look at, and normally sold in museums and fine gift stores.

2775 Dundas St. W., (one and a half blocks east of Keele St.), Toronto.
Tel: 416-763-6275 or 1-800-416-0590
Hours: Call for 2002 sale dates and hours.

CANALITE HOME FASHION SALE

Over 200 patterns of high quality linens and bath accessories to choose from at 35% to 80% off at this home fashion sale. Their famous Canadian made white goose down duvet, queen size, 30 oz., is on sale for $140.00. They carry 350-thread count damask combed cotton sateen sheet sets for only $120.99. A great sale for picking up clearance bedding and bath items below cost.

52 West Beaver Creek Rd. Unit 8, (north of Hwy. #7, west of Leslie St.) Richmond Hill.
Tel: 905-886-2370.
Hours: Monday to Saturday 10 a.m. to 6 p.m., Thursday till 7:00 p.m.
Call for 2002-3 sale dates.

fabric and linen

CHUSHING TEXTILES
440 Queen St. W., (west of Spadina Ave.), Toronto.
Tel: 416-504-9069
Hours: M.-Sat. 9-7

DEBLINS LINENS SUPERSTORE
39 Orfus Rd. (south of 401, west off Dufferin St.), North York.
Tel: 416-782-2910
Hours: M. to Sat. 10 - 6, Thu. 10 - 9, Sun. 12 - 6

DESIGNER FABRIC OUTLET
1360 Queen St. W. (west of Dufferin St.), Toronto.
Tel: 416-531-2810
Hours: M. to W. 9:30 - 6, Thu. & F. 9:30 - 9, Sat 9:30 - 6:30

DOWNTOWN DUVETS & LINENS 📷
530 Adelaide St. W., Basement (H. Brown building, just east of
Bathurst St.), Toronto.
Tel: 416-703-3777
Hours: Call for specific dates and times of Warehouse sales.

DOWN UNDER LINENS - WAREHOUSE OUTLET 📷
As always, this outlet continues to be a great spot to stock up on linens, and
right now they are also clearing out a wide variety of in stock beds, as well as
duvets. Their Canadian white goose down duvet with 35 oz. of down is currently priced at $139 - considerably less than the competition. As well, we
saw a terrific collection of cotton duvet covers priced at $49.99 - regularly
priced at up to $149. Caution, however - their prices are not always well
marked, so it's wise to double check the price - it's often lower than you
think! Two annual clearance sales: first week of November and May.
    444 Yonge St. (College Park), Toronto.
    Tel: 416-598-2184
    Hours: M. to W. 10 – 6, Thu. & F. 10 – 7, Sat 10 – 6, Sun. 12 - 5
    5170 Dixie Road (south of the 401), Mississauga.
    Tel: 905-624-5854
    Hours: M. to Wed. 10 - 6, Thu. & F. 10 - 8, Sat. 10-6, Sun. 12 – 5
    5221 Highway #7 (SW corner McCowan and #7), Markham.
    Tel: 905-305-9496
    Hours: M. to Fri. 10 - 8, Sat. 10-6, Sun. 12-5   See advertisement on page A7

fabric and linen

DREAMS DOWNEY DUVETS - FACTORY OUTLET

215 Spadina Ave., Toronto.
Tel: 416-596-8489 or Toll free: 1-800-265-7104
Thornhill Square, 300 John St. (at Bayview Ave.), Thornhill.
Hours: M. to F. 10 - 9, Sat. 10 - 6, Sun. 12 - 5
Call for other locations.

EASTERN TEXTILES

164 Bentworth Ave. (E. off Caledonia Rd., & S. of Hwy. 401), Toronto.
Tel: 416-783-1119
Hours: M. to F. 8:30 - 4:30, Sat. 10 - 2:30

FABRIC CLEARANCE CENTRE

Another great find in the city for fabric with a good assortment of home
decor fabrics for drapery and upholstery as well as foam, leather and a huge
assortment of vinyl with everything neat and arranged by colour too.
www.fabricclearance.com

Location: 4884 Dufferin St., Unit 6, (three lights north of Finch Ave.,
west side), Downsview.
Tel: 416-665-4647
Hours: M.-F. 9-6, Sat. 9-5

FINE DESIGN FABRICS - DRAPERY AND UPHOLSTERY OUTLET

A great selection of upholstery weight fabrics, chenilles, silk and drapery fabrics, with in-stock fabrics starting at $5.99 to $35.00/yard.

410 Chesswood Dr. #A (west of Dufferin St. and south off Finch Ave.),
Downsview.
Tel: 416-636-4904
Hours: M. to F. 9 - 5, Sat. 10 – 4

THE FINNISH PLACE 🔥

You will feel like you're in Finland as you walk into this small store. Unique
items that include tableware in Arabia patterns will be on sale at 30 to 50%
off. Lovely quality and thirty years of design experience create a warm ambience for this shopping excursion.

5463 Yonge St. (three blocks south of Finch Ave.), Toronto.
Tel: 416-222-7575
Hours: Call for 2002 sale date and hours.

---

fabric and linen

HALTON LINEN COMPANY
481 North Service Rd. West (between Dorval Rd. and Fourth Line),
Oakville.
Tel: 905-847-2274
Hours: M.-F. 10-5:30, Sat. 9-6, and Sunday noon to 5 p.m.

HOME GOODS & MORE INC.
Just opened, a new outlet for all your linen needs and more. Bed in Bags start
at only $40, Cannon bath towels are 3 for $12, 7 hand towels only $10 and 6
wash cloths only $5. Huge deals on 5' x 8' area rugs regularly $179 for only
$50 and 8' x 11' rugs only $80. Percale sheets sets are from $15 up. There are
lots of pillows, tablecloths and other gift ideas. Our big purchase was 12 pairs
of ladies socks for only $8. These outlets are worth several trips as stock
changes weekly.
6 Mars Rd., (off Hwy. #27, south of Steeles Ave., north of Albion Rd.)
Etobicoke. Tel: 416-742-3403
780 Birchmount Rd., Scarborough.
Tel: 416-750-4309
3905 Keele St., Unit 2, Toronto.
Tel: 416-633-5928
1285 Kennedy Rd., Unit 3, Scarborough.
Tel: 416-757-3667.
Hours: M.-W. 10 a.m. to 7 p.m., Thu., Fri. 10 a.m. to 8 p.m., Sat. 10 a.m. to 6
p.m. and Sun. noon to 5 p.m.

LA CACHE - CLEARANCE STORE
This small jewel is tucked into one of Hamilton's shopping malls, and is a haven
for those who love the colours and designs of La Cache's table and bed linens
and clothing. All merchandise is at least 50% off their regular retail prices, and
consists of ends-of-lines, leftover stock, damaged items and odds and ends.
Stock changes constantly, and right now you'll find some spring clothes from
last year, as well as children's winter clothing. All linens and clothing are 100%
cotton made in India. We particularly like their tablecloths - and at this price,
you can afford several! Last season's damaged goods, 75% off retail.
Jackson Square Mall, 2 King Street West, Hamilton.
Tel: 905-528-3270
Hours: M. to Sat. 10 – 5, Sun. 12 – 5

---

fabric and linen

LEN'S MILL STORE

Len's has one of the largest ranges of home decorating fabrics we've seen. This includes upholstery and quilting fabrics, as well as drapery hardware and notions at very competitive prices. As well, you'll discover a huge assortment of hand knitting yarns. And if you need hosiery for the family, check out their brand name hosiery at bargain prices. Many locations in southwestern Ontario, with a superstore in Guelph.

Eight locations in Ontario.
Tel: Toll free: 1-888-536-7645 for a complete list,
Website: www.lensmill.com.
Hours: M., T., W. and Sat. 10- 5; Thu. and Fri. 10- 9, Sun. 12-5

MACDONALD FABER FABRICS – 💲

Just in for fall, cut velvet chenilles, great for cushions and other home decorating ideas, all $8.00 per meter, regular $35.00, imported from Europe. Also available faux furs as low as $15.99 per meter. Try some of their great decorating ideas – purchase an uncovered, quality foam cube for $60.00 and choose from their many fabrics to create the cover for your ottoman. High quality, imported non-pilling fleece available for only $12.99 per meter, regularly $39.00 elsewhere. Get ready for next summer and purchase some outdoor fabric while you are there for only $8.00 per meter.

952 Queen Street West, Toronto.
Tel: 416-922-6000
Hours: Monday to Friday 9 a.m. to 5 p.m., Saturday 10 a.m. to 5 p.m.

MISSISSAUGA BEDDING SUPERSTORE
-UPPER CANADA SOAP & CANDLE MAKERS

Grand Re-Opening Summer 2000 with a huge open concept design. Look for duvets, sheets and towels, kitchen and bathroom accessories, bath and body products, candles and accessories – with new inventory arriving daily. Great place for gifts at outlet store prices.

1510 Caterpillar Road (north of The Queensway, off Dixie Road), Mississauga.
Tel: 905 - 897-1710
Hours: M. – F. 10-5, Sat. 10-4, Sun. closed

PATRICIAN LINENS

Enjoy savings of up to 40% off on high quality European bedding, bath and tabletop products. If you love fine linens, you'll enjoy the 400 thread count Egyptian 100% cotton duvet covers, bed sets, mohair blankets, linen tablecloths and much more. This outlet has now moved into a larger space making shopping even more customer friendly.

   1875 Leslie Street, unit 20   (north of York Mills), Toronto.
   Tel: 416-444-1100
   Hours: M.-F. 10-6; Sat. 10-5; Sun. noon to 5

See advertisement on page A26

SEW RIGHT   -   MASTER RIGHTS FACTORY SALE – 🏠

Love linens on sale? Visit the new location for this sale of comforters, Bed in a Bag, duvet covers, tablecloths, cushions and more. Bed in a Bag starts at $49.99, so at this price you can afford to update your home!

   11 Director Court (north of Steeles Ave., west of Hwy. #400), Vaughan.
   Tel: 905-850-6131
   Hours: Call for sale dates and times.

SUREWAY TRADING - SILK WHOLESALERS

Sharon's favorite for decades, this outlet imports a mind boggling array of silks with every quality, weight, texture and colour imaginable at excellent prices. At the end of the month they are moving just around the corner but keeping this phone number - call ahead.

   111 Peter St., Suite 212, (east of Spadina Ave. and north off King St.), Toronto.
   Tel: 416 -596-1887
   Hours: M. to F. 10 - 5:30, Sat. 11 - 3:30

Coffee (n.), a person who is coughed upon.

---

fabric and linen

THE LACE PLACE

This is a real find for anyone looking for high quality upholstery, fabric and trims. The latest fabric from VIP and Cranston Works starts at $4.99/yard, and trimming and fringes are 20% off retail. Beautiful Spanish tassels and fringe to match. Some upholstery fabrics were $10.00/yard, regularly $45.00/yard. and their Christmas fabrics start arriving in August, in lots of time for any big events. With over 7000 square feet of retail space in the warehouse, you should find what you are looking for.

1698 Bayly Street (take the 401 east to Brock Road south, and turn right on Bayly Street), Pickering.
Tel: 905-831-5223
Hours: M.-F. 10 - 9, Sat. 10 - 6, Sun. noon - 5
See advertisement on page A22

WESTPOINT STEVENS FACTORY OUTLET SALE

Time to restock the linen closet with this great outlet sale on for only two days. They are clearing out hundreds of last year's famous name brand products and discontinued items.

All their duvet covers, comforters, blankets, bed skirts and shams are on sale, in assorted patterns, sizes and colours from only $20. Sheets sets from 180 thread count up start at $15 for twin to $30 for king. Their beautiful bath towels are $3, $5 and $7 with face cloths only $1. We bought several bath sheets for the cottage for only $10 each.

5800 Avebury Rd., (first street west of Hurontario St., south off Britannia Rd.), Mississauga.
Tel: 905-712-8999.
Hours: Call for 2003 sale date and times
See advertisement on page A17

WIN WIN BOUTIQUE

Are you interested in buying fabrics, notions, seconds and samples at rock bottom prices? Come to Linda Lundström Inc. head office where they're selling fabric and remnants by the metere, cuttings by the bagful, damaged seconds and development samples (oops we all make mistakes) by the armload – all at great prices. Inventory changes regularly.

255 Wicksteed Ave. Front entrance (free parking at rear)
Tel: 416-423-4560 ext. 300 for directions and information
Hours: Every Thursday throughout the year (statutory holidays excepted)

leisure time

- Arts, Crafts & Books
- Toys, Party Novelties & Packaging
- Florists, Gift Basket

Ransom

arts, crafts and books

AYUS OUTLET SALE 🏮

This importer of eclectic handicrafts is holding their first outlet sale. We found amazing items for the home that included beaded frames, incense burners, wonderful candles, fabric covered boxes and hand-carved wooden jewellery boxes. Our teenager thought this was the coolest sale ever, and I was also intrigued by the array of exotic items. Most items were under $10, and candles considerably less.

> Sale will be held in the Scents Alive Factory Outlet Store at 1300 Alness Street (NW corner of Steeles Ave. and Alness St.), Toronto.
> Tel: 905-760-7945
> Hours: Call for 2002 sale dates, location and hours.

THE BOOK DEPOT INC.

> 340 Welland Ave., (QEW west, exit at Niagara St. and remain on the South Service Rd. - turn right Welland Ave.), St. Catharines.
> Toll free: 1-800-801-7193
> Hours: M. to W. 9 - 6, Thu. & F. 9 - 9, Sat. 9 - 5

CRAFT TREE

With summer nearly over and the kids are bored, try a visit to this store. They carry pom- poms, beads, felt, fun foam, clay pots, wood turnings, decorative paint, silk and dried flowers, ribbon, feathers etc., and are able to keep prices low. Weekly specials are often featured on paints, brushes and craft supplies. Classes and birthday parties with a "designed for you craft", meal and loot bags are regular features.

> 327 Bronte Street South, White Oaks Plaza, Milton.
> Tel: 905-875-4917.
> Other locations in Tillsonburg 519-688-9688, St. Thomas 519-637-2723 and Woodstock 519-539-2802.
> Hours: Summer hours Monday to Wednesday 9:00 a.m. to 6:00 p.m., Thursday and Friday 9 a.m. to 8 p.m, Saturday 10 a.m. to 5 p.m. Call for fall hours.

CRAFTER'S DECOR
226 Queen Street South (south of Hwy. #401, take Mississauga Rd. exit, then left and third light), Streetsville.
Tel: 905-567-9795
Hours: T. & W. 10 - 6, Thu. & F. 10 - 7, Sat. 10 - 5, Sun. 12 - 4 open additional hours from September - December, call for details.

CRAFTERS MARKETPLACES (THE)
167 Queen St. S. (south of Hwy. 401, take Mississauga Rd. exit, then left at third light), Streetsville.
Tel: 905-632-1990
Call for other locations.

EPILEPSY ONTARIO – ANNUAL ART SALE
Epilepsy Ontario's ANNUAL ART SALE may well be the sale of a lifetime, for new collectors and seasoned professionals alike. Art work, which is priced at less than one third of the appraised value, includes world class artists such as Pablo Picasso, Stephen Snake, The Group of Seven's A.J. Casson, R.G. Miller, Dubi Arie, Salvador Dali, Jose RoyBal, and many more Originals and Limited Edition Prints. Proceeds support the work and research of this most deserving organization.
Promenade Mall, Bathurst and Centre Street, Suite 308 Thornhill.
Tel: 905-764-5099.
November 15 – 21, 2002

HAMPSTEAD HOUSE BOOKS - OFF-PRICE OUTLET
80 Doncaster Ave. (east off Yonge St, north of Steeles Ave.), Thornhill.
Tel: 905-881-0607
Hours: M. to F. 9 - 4

INTICRAFTS - IMPORTERS STORES
372A Queen St. W., Toronto.
Tel: 416-593-0197
Hours: M. to Sat. 11 - 7, Sun. 12 – 6
Call for other location.

arts, crafts and books

LYNRICH ARTS
73 Doncaster Ave. (Yonge and Steeles area), Thornhill.
Tel: 905-771-0411
Hours: Open 7 days per week - Call for hours.

MALABAR
14 McCaul St. (just N. of Queen St. W.), Toronto.
Tel: 416-598-2581
Hours: M. to F. 10 - 6, Sat. 10 - 5

MANUFACTURERS ART SALE 📇
481 Hanlan Road (west of Weston Road, just north of Steeles Ave.),
Woodbridge.
Tel: 905 - 850-0375
Hours: Call for sale dates and time.

MARY MAXIM 📇
Canada's best known craft mail order house and retail distribution centre
offers a wide variety of knitting yarns, needlework kits, general crafts,
and quilting fabrics. Come in to select from the largest variety of cross
stitch kits in Ontario. Mary Maxim's private label sweater and afghan kits
are an exceptional value too!
Don't miss the Clearance Room which offers savings from all departments.
The first Tuesday of every month is CLUB 50 DAY, where all customers 50 or
over save 20% on all products!
Great reason to drive to Paris - Ontario that is. Where you can discover
"Crafts" Life's Little Pleasures.
75 Scott Ave., (north of town off Hwy # 24A), Paris.
Tel. 1-888-442-2266
www.marymaxim.com

See advertisement on page A28

MASKERADE MANOR COSTUME RENTALS
If you are attending a costume party soon, this is the place to visit. They have
over 2,000 costumes for rent and a large selection of wigs, make-up and
accessories. My brother rented two costumes, with all the accessories for
under $50 each. Go early for the best selection and have some fun in the
haunted dark room!
18 Queen St. East, (West on Hwy. #401, north on Hwy. #24 to Queen St.,

---

turn right . They are just beyond the third traffic light.) Cambridge, Ontario.

Tel: 519-658-6260; Toll Free: 1-888-277-Mask

Hours for October: Monday to Friday noon to 8 p.m., Saturday 9 a.m. to 4 p.m., Sunday noon to 5

Balance of the year: Sat. 9-4; Mon. to Fri. by appointment.

MINNOW BOOKS

1251 Northside Rd. (North of QEW, between Walkers Line and Guelph Line off Mainway), Burlington.

Toll free: 1-800-263-5210

Hours: Thu. 8-8; Fri. 8 - 6;. Sat. 8 - 2.

NATIONAL BOOK SERVICE SALE

25 Kodiak Crescent (north of Sheppard Avenue, west of Allan Road), North York.

Tel: 416-630-2950 or

Toll free: 1-800-387-3178

PSH - THE POTTERY SUPPLY HOUSE

1120 Speers Rd., (between 3rd and 4th Lines, on the south side), Oakville.

Tel: 905-827-1129 or

Toll free: 1- 800-465-8544

Hours: M. to F. 8:30 - 5, Sat. 9 – 1 (July and August closed on Saturdays)

SANDYLION STICKER DESIGNS

While the kids are off school and wondering what to do, pick up some stickers, sticker books, albums at 50 to 80% off retail prices. You will find a huge selection of seconds and ends of lines of rolls, strips, kits and more here to help pass away March break with arts and crafts.

400 Cochrane Drive, (rear of building, south of Hwy. #7, west of Woodbine Ave.), Markham.

Tel: 905-475-6771

Hours: Monday to Friday 9 a.m. to 6 p.m., Saturday 9 a.m. to 4 p.m., Sunday 11 a.m. to 4 p.m.

arts, crafts and books

SPINRITE FACTORY OUTLET
230 Elma St. W., (at the stoplight take Wallace Ave. S. off Hwy. 86 to
Elma), Listowel.
Tel: 519- 291-3951
Hours: M. to F. 9 - 6, Sat. 9 – 5, Sun. 11-5

TANDY LEATHER COMPANY - OUTLET STORES
Most people will recognize this Canadian distributor of leathercraft goods and
assorted craft supplies - there are dozens of retail stores across Canada. At
their distribution centres, shoppers will find extra savings on clearances of
end-of-lines etc.
20 Brock St. (north of Essa Rd. and west off Anne St.), Barrie.
Tel: 705-728-6501
1654 Victoria Park Avenue, Scarborough.
Tel : 416-757-1392
Hours: M. to F. 9 - 5, Sat. 9 – 4

TRINITY COLLEGE BOOK SALE 📖
The 27th annual, well-loved sale of used books including rare, special and just
plain honest good books opens Friday for 4 _ days. Last year's sale offered finds
from more than 2,400 tightly packed, well-sorted cartons of books on every
imaginable topic. All books are donated, no library discards and all labour is vol-
unteer, with all proceeds supporting the library. This sale is addictive.
Trinity College, 6 Hoskin Avenue (upstairs in Seeley Hall). If you are
taking transit, get off at either the Museum subway stop, or the St. George
stop, Toronto.
Tel: 416-978-6750
Call for hours and date.

WAREHOUSE BOOK SALE 📖
With thousands of publishers overstocks and remainders priced at up to 90%
off original price, you may be able to find some great gifts, or just some won-
derful reading for yourself. 100% of the profits go to the Crohn's and Colitis
Foundation of Canada, so this is an even better reason to shop at this sale.
120 Duffield Drive (west off Kennedy Road north of 14th
Avenue), Markham.
Tel: 416-920-5055
Hours: Call for hours and dates.

toys, party novelties and packaging

AVONLEA TRADITIONS INC. WAREHOUSE SALE 🏠

This company makes the wonderful dolls, collectibles and other gifts based on Canada's most famous storybook character. The sale features Klutz Activity kits and books at 30% off, Dorling Kindersley books, stickers and science kits at 40% off and the famous Anne of Green Gables dolls at up to 80% off. The Fairy Tale Classic porcelain dolls are 25% off and Maple North Dolls of Canada are up to 75% off. Great place to pick up gifts for all the girls on your list.

> 17075 Leslie St. Unit 8, (3 blocks south of Davis Dr.) Newmarket.
> Tel: 905-853-1777.
> Hours: Call for sale dates. Monday to Saturday 9:30 a.m. to 5 p.m.

ALIRON MARKETING

Chock full of gifts ..... Most items are under $20 and prices include tax. Prices generally are 40% to 60% off retail. They are not open to the public, but you can visit their web site and place an order –
www.alironmarketing.com

> 261 Trowers Road (south of Hwy. 7, west of Hwy 400), Woodbridge
> Tel: Toll free: 1-877-325-4766
> Call for hours.

BAGS OF FUN

> 94 George Street (QEW to Trafalgar Road, south to the Lakeshore and west two blocks). Oakville.
> Tel: 905-337-2247
> Hours: Closed M., T. to Sat. 9:30 - 5:30

CANADIAN HOBBYCRAFT - MANUFACTURERS OUTLET

> 140 Applewood Cres. (north of Hwy. 7, west off Jane St.), Concord.
> Tel: 905-738-6556
> Hours: M. to F. 8:30 – 5

toys, party novelties and packaging

COLT-PAK CONTAINERS

If you are moving soon we have found a great packaging warehouse. They offer fabulous deals on moving cartons from $2.00, wardrobe containers, tape, bubble wrap, newsprint or just about anything that is needed to handle a move.

151 Sterling Rd (2 blocks west of Lansdowne, north side of Dundas St.) Toronto.

Tel: 416-535-7234.

Hours: Monday to Friday 9 a.m. to 5 p.m.

CREATIVE BAG-STARLIGHT RIBBON

Gift wrapping? Point of sale packaging? Maybe a wedding bonbonierre that has to wrapped , a great organza bag, or a unique loot bag, they have it all at their packaging warehouse. Between the 6,000 sq.ft. warehouse in Mississauga full of ribbon and the 3500 sq.ft. warehouse in Downsview they have all your packaging needs covered at discounted prices. If you mention the Shoestring shopping guide you will receive a free packaging gift.

880 Steeprock Drive (Allan Expressway and Sheppard Ave. area), Downsview.

Tel: 416-631-6444

Hours: Creative Bag – M, W. and F. 9-6, Thurs. 9-8, Sat 9-5, Sun. noon - 5

Starlite Ribbon - 975 Pacific Gate (North of Britannia Road, west of Tomken), Mississauga

Tel: 905 - 670-2651

Hours: M- F 8:30 - 4:30, Sat 9 – 5

Website: www.creativebag.com

EASY PACK CORPORATION

This time of year usually means a lot of people on the move – either returning from university, getting ready for the summer at the cottage, or moving to a new house. In any case, it often means packing boxes. Why not pack with used cartons? At this manufacturer, used cartons start for as little as .95 each. Of course they also sell new cartons, as well as packing material such as bubble wrap, newsprint and foam chips. Definitely less expensive than buying from rental shops.

60 McPherson Street (south of Hwy. 407, west off Warden Ave.), Markham

Tel: 905-470-1261

EVERGREEN PACKAGING INC.

70 Clayson Road, (North of Hwy 401, west of Jane, North of Wilson Ave),
Toronto.
  Tel: 416-740-4345
  Hours: M. - Sat. 10 - 5
  Call for sale dates.

GANZ WAREHOUSE SALE 🏠

  1 Pearce Road (North of Steeles Ave., west of Weston Road)
  Hours: Late Nov. - mid. Dec. T.- F. 11 – 7, Sat. & Sun. noon to 5.

HENRY LIMITED 🏠

  1 Head St., (west of Hamilton, south of Hwy. 5, north of Hwy.99), Dundas.
  Tel: 905-628-2231
  Hours: Please call for hours.

LET'S CELEBRATE!

If you are entertaining over the coming season, you'll find some of the guaranteed lowest prices around on all kinds of holiday tableware items, cups, plates, napkins, table covers and balloons to make your party a success. Right now they have the entire selection of boxed holiday cards at 75% off list with over 300 styles to choose from, and in addition, their entire selection of gift-wrap is 25% off. We particularly liked the fibre optic Christmas tree for only $16.99. Lots of gift sets, Christmas mugs, photo albums and more.
  280 Kingston Rd., (east of Harwood Rd.) Ajax.
  Tel: 905 683-3532
  4 Kennedy Rd., (Queen St. and Kennedy Rd.), Brampton.
  Tel: 905-457-4606
  7171 Yonge St. (just north of Steeles Ave.), Thornhill.
  Tel: 905 771-9438
  1225 Dundas St. E. (Dundas St., west of Dixie), Misissauga,
  Tel: 905 275-3799
  Call 905 761-1249 for more locations.
  Hours: Open 7 days a week, Monday to Friday 9:30 a.m. to 9 p.m.,
  Saturday 9:30 a.m. to 6 p.m., Sunday 10 a.m. to 6 p.m.

---

toys, party novelties and packaging

MARKA CANADA - CLEARANCE OUTLET
4500 Dixie Rd., Unit 11B, (south of Eglinton Ave.), Mississauga.
Tel: 905 - 238-6599
Hours: M. to F. 9 - 5

MATTEL TOY CLUB
6155 Freemont Blvd., (2 lights west of Hwy. 10 on Britannia Rd.),
Mississauga .
Tel: 905-501-5147 (Outlet Hotline)
Hours: T. and W. 10 – 5, Th. -F. 10 –9, Sat. 10 - 5.

MIKO TOY WAREHOUSE 🏠
Lots of deals here on brand name toys like Crayola, Little Tikes, Fisher-Price,
Mattel and Hot Wheels at some of the lowest prices around. There is a huge
selection of Golden books, puzzles, games, trains and hockey sets, stocking
stuffers, radio control vehicles, girls dress up items and doll accessories. They
also have a special program for companies and groups purchasing children's
Christmas party presents. Call for more information.
60 East Beaver Creek Road, (north of Hwy #7, just west of Hwy
404), Richmond Hill.
Tel: 905-771-8714
Hours: Sept. 28 to Dec. 22 (not open Monday or Tuesday)
Wednesday 10:00 a.m. - 4:00 p.m. Thur & Fri 10:00 a.m. - 8:00 p.m.
Saturday 10:00 a.m. - 5:00 p.m. Sunday 11:00 a.m. - 5:00 p.m.
See advertisement on page A18 A19

NOAH'S ARK INDOOR PLAYLAND
5004 Timberlea Blvd., Units #9 & 10 (Eglinton Ave. E. to Tomken
Road, right on Timberlea Blvd. and left at the first lights), Mississauga.
Tel: 905-629-7946
Hours: Parties are available weekdays after school and evenings, Sat.
and Sun. morning and afternoons

NORAMPAC - BOX OUTLET
7700 Keele St., (west side just south of Hwy. 7), Concord.
Tel: 416-663-6340
Hours: M. to F. 7-4 closed holidays.

toys, party novelties and packaging

PACKAGING WORLD

Have you ever tried sending a parcel overseas, only to realize you lacked adequate packaging or the appropriate box? This wholesale outlet will sell you everything you need from boxes, bubble wrap, tape, corrugated wrap, labels and whatever it takes to make your move manageable.

830 Steeprock Dr. (just off the Allen Expressway between Sheppard and Finch Ave.), Downsview.
Tel: 416-631-7441
Hours: M. to F. 9 – 5

PARTY PACKAGERS

Your one-stop Party Store for endless supplies of Toys, Loot, Party accessories and much, much more. All under one roof! This awesome store has everything to make your special event an absolutely memorable one.

Join them on-line at www.partypackagers.com and become a member of their Party Club. Membership advantages include Free Birthday Gifts, Great Savings, Contest Prizes and so much more!!
Sign up today!!!

1225 Finch Ave. West (east of Keele Street), North York
Tel: 416-631-7688
Other locations in Ancaster, Mississauga, Toronto, Scarborough and Ajax.
Visit website for more details.

QSP/READER'S DIGEST WAREHOUSE SALE 🛍

Bigger than ever this year! The annual Christmas warehouse sale with up to 80% off on wrapping paper, Christmas ornaments, candles, mugs, gift baskets, stocking stuffers, Reader's Digest Books, electronics, toys, plush, chocolate, chocolate and more chocolate.
Cash, Visa and Interac accepted.

442 Passmore Ave. (south of Steeles and west of Markham Rd.), Scarborough.
Tel: 416-299-4450
Hours: Call for sale dates and hours.

toys, party novelties and packaging

REGAL GREETINGS AND GIFTS

1147 Bellamy Rd., Scarborough.

Tel: 416-425-5858

Hours: M. to W. & F. 9:30 - 5:30, Thu. 9:30 - 8, Sat. 9 – 5

Call for other locations.

RIZCO TOY & GIFT WAREHOUSE SALE 🔲

(October 17, 2002 – December 24, 2002

This is the fun sale!! Don't miss out on these enormous savings of up to 70%. This sale stocks a variety of items, including toys, children's and educational books, cook books, stationery, bags, small electronics, business and travel accessories, giftware, household items, stocking stuffers, Christmas decorations, planners, educational software/computer games, and much more. You'll find clearance, Factory Over-Runs, discontinued, close outs, bankruptcy and current season merchandise. Visit their new Toronto Warehouse Outlet at 130 Orfus Rd. They usually open numerous locations around the province. For the one closest to you, hours of operation and additional information, call the Rizco information line toll free number listed below.

130 Orfus Rd., (at Caledonia, just south of the Yorkdale Shopping Centre off Dufferin.), Toronto.

Tel: 1-877-305-3775 for hours and nearest location.

Payment method: Visa, MC, Interac Direct Payment and cash.

See advertisement on page A21

Flabbergasted (adj.), appalled over how much weight you have gained.

---

toys, party novelties and packaging

ROYAL SPECIALTY SALES 🏠
11 Industrial St (five blocks south of Eglinton. Ave. and east of Laird Dr.), Toronto.
Tel: 416-423-1133

SAMKO SALES - TOY AND GIFT WAREHOUSE OUTLET
Shoppers can expect a vast selection of name brand toys and gifts at excellent pricing (most below wholesale). Not generally open to the public, this copy of Shoestring will allow you entrance and please leave any kids under the age of 16 at home.

11 Peel Ave. (turn N. on Gladstone Ave., off Queen St. W.), Toronto.
Tel: 416-532-1114
Hours: Oct. 2nd. –Dec. 22nd., Wed. 10-4, Thu., Fri. 10-8, Sun. 11-5
(Closed Mon. & Tues.)

See advertisement on page A18 A19

STUDIO SPECIALTIES 🏠
289 Bridgeland Ave. (W. off Dufferin St., under the 401), Toronto.
Tel: 416-787-1813
Hours: M. to F. 9 – 5

florists, gift baskets

BASKITS WAREHOUSE SALE 🏺
750 Birchmount Rd., Units 51 & 52 (south of Eglinton Ave.), Scarborough.
Tel: 416-755-1100

CREST FLORAL STUDIO 🏺
An annual sale, not to be missed of glassware, ceramics, ribbon, baskets, artificial flowers, giftware, Christmas ornaments and décor items. It is their oops! it's chipped, oops! it a leftover, oops! it's a lemon, or oops! an overstocked sale. They are also having a one week special on their beautiful British Columbia hydrangeas shipped direct from their BC growers.
593 Mount Pleasant Road, Toronto.
Tel: 416-487-0491. Call for sale date.
Hours: 10 a.m. to 5 p.m.

FLOWER DEPOT
2902 Bloor St. W., Etobicoke.
Tel: 416 - 236-8273
Call for other locations.

GIFT-PAK/DAREE IMPORTS AND SALES LTD. 🏺
Always a favourite when assembling a gift basket or stuffing a stocking. These two companies at one location are at the top of our list with a wide variety of cosmetics, bath and hair care products, as well as a fine lineup of portion packed gourmet foods, fine chocolates, candles, napkins and all the wrappings, bows and baskets to bring it all together. Warehouse sale in November. Call for details.
5486 Gorvan Dr. (south of Highway 401, east off Tomken Rd. on to Brevik Place, left to Gorvan Dr.), Mississauga.
Tel: 905-624-3359
Hours: M. to Wed. and Fri. 9-4, Thurs. 9-7, Sat. 10-3. Closed on Sat. during the summer.

See advertisement on page A8

GRATRIX GARDEN LILIES
3714 Vasey Rd., (take Hwy. 400 about 40 kms. north of Barrie, exit #141 and go west about 3 km., on north side), Coldwater.
Tel: 705-835-6794
Web site: www.bconnex.net\gratlily
Hours: Open daily 8 - 8 until Oct. 31st.

florists, gift baskets

LIB & IDO'S ROSE EMPORIUM

For a wonderful selection of roses, this florist carries 30 to 50 different varieties and colours of fresh cut roses. Some are local and some are imported, but they do have the most wonderful selection around. Prices start at $25.00 a dozen. We found the service excellent and there is delivery in the GTA.

204 Dupont St., Toronto.

Tel: 416 -922-9909

Hours: Please call for seasonal hours.

REGAL CONFECTIONS 📠

175 Britannia Road, Mississauga.

Tel: 905-507-6868

Hours: 6 weeks before Christmas, open M. to F. 8:30 - 4:30, Sat. 10 - 3

ROSES ONLY

Roses only has an incredible selection of roses. All are farm fresh with up to 200 varieties to choose from. Renowned in Toronto for its wedding work, Roses Only offers 24 roses bridal bouquet for $85.00. The staff will work with you to design your special wedding day and to stay within your budget. They also have a wide variety of cut flowers at super prices.

8 Market Street, (south of Front St. west of Jarvis St.), Toronto.

Tel: 416-594-6678

Hours: Mon. 8:30 - 2:00, Tues – Fri. 8:30-6:00, Saturday 8:30 - 3:00
Sunday closed.

WHAT A BASKET!

There's still lots of time to order a customized basket for friends, colleagues or even yourself! We ordered several last year as gifts, and were delighted with the quality and price. Choose from dozens of baskets filled with gourmet treats, or find everything you need to make your own. Gift baskets also available at their Square One Christmas location on the lower level.

6705 Tomken Rd., Units 5 & 6 (Tomken & Derry Rds. area), Mississauga.

Tel: 905-670-8056

Hours: M. to F. 8:30 - 4:30, Sat. 10 - 3

florists, gift baskets

WHOLESALE FLORISTS
This superstore has an unusual concept. By becoming a member for $29.95 a year; you receive wholesale prices on all your floral purchases. Non-members also buy at competitive prices, but a membership allows your family exceptional value. The savings are particularly impressive if you are planning a wedding or other event where flowers are centre stage! Browse their 1000 sq. ft. walk in cooler for both imported and local flowers. www.wholesalefloralgroup.com

55 Colossus Drive, Unit 128, (Hwy. 7 & Weston Road) Woodbridge.
Tel: 905 - 851-3001
Hours: M.- F. 9-5 , Sat. 10-6, Sun. 10-5

WILD FLOWER FARM
R.R.#3 (between Schomberg & Nobleton on the first road W. of Hwy. 27, just N. of the 17th Sideroad), Schomberg.
Tel: 905-859-0286
Hours: M. to Sun. 10 - 6

More Bible revisions by minors
Actual responses to bible questions on a test given to elementary school kids.

•Jesus was born because Mary had an immaculate contraption.

•Jesus enunciated the Golden Rule, which says to do one to others before they do one to you. He also explained, a man doth not live by sweat alone.

•The people who followed the lord were called the 12 decibels.

•The epistles were the wives of the apostles.

•St. Paul cavorted to Christianity. He preached holy acrimony, which another name for marriage.

business

• Office Supplies, computers & Electronics

office supplies, computers & electronics

CITIZEN ELECTRONICS
455 Gordon Baker Rd. (one light south of Victoria Park Ave. and Steeles Ave.), Willowdale.
Tel: 416 -499-5611
Hours: M. to F. 8 - 5

DAY-TIMER OF CANADA
9515 Montrose Rd., Niagara Falls.
Tel: 905-356-8020 or 1-800-465-5501
Hours: M. to F. 8 - 5

THE ELECTRONICS OUTLET
6200 Edwards Blvd. (North East corner of 401 & Hwy # 10), Mississauga.
Tel: 905-672-8616.
Hours: M. to F. 10 a.m. to 6 p.m. Closed Sat. & Sun

IBM WAREHOUSE OUTLET
It's not often you get a chance to pick up world class technology at outlet prices, but that's exactly what IBM is doing at this location - when we dropped in to the outlet store recently, we bought two systems absolutely loaded with memory and power for an unbelievable price - so drop in for Big Blue's bargains on new and refurbished products that include computers, monitors, printers, peripherals, accessories, software and more. Quantities are limited but..... isn't it time to upgrade your system?
4175 - 14th Avenue, (East of Warden Ave., South of Highway 7), Markham.
Tel: 905 - 316-7777
Hours: M - F 10 – 6, Sat. 10 - 5

IBM HOME COMPUTING STORE
3300 Highway 7 West Seven and 400 Centre, Vaughan.
Tel: 905-660-9333
Hours: Open 7 days a week – 10-6

LITEMOR

325 Deerhide Cres. (west of Hwy. 400 on Finch Ave. take Arrow Rd. south), Weston.
Tel: 416-745-3806
Hours: M. to F. 8 – 5

MAXIUM WAREHOUSE DIRECT – REFURBISHED COMPUTERS

Maxium Warehouse Direct offers quality refurbished PC Products at prices you can afford. With Tier 1 brand names like IBM, Dell, Compaq, HP and Toshiba, Maxium has a wide range of desktops, notebooks, monitors, printers and peripherals in stock. To ensure that quality is of the highest standard, Maxium certified technicians put each piece of equipment through extensive diagnostic testing and refurbishment, prior to any sale.

Pricing that can be as low as 90% off original MSRP, combined with a 30 day full exchange warranty, provides you with the comfort that you are buying value when you buy from Maxium. Stop in at the warehouse outlet or visit them online at "www.maxium.net/warehousedirect" and you'll see where technology and value come together.

30 Vogell Rd., Markham, Ont.
Tel: 905-780-9514

See advertisement on page A1

MEI

310 Alden Rd., Markham.
Tel: 905-475-8444
Web site;www.mansoorelectronics.com
Call for sale dates and hours.

PLAYBACK ELECTRONICS 📱

358 Flint Rd. (north of Finch Ave. west off Dufferin St. on Martin Ross Rd. to Flint), Downsview.
Tel: 416-661-7781
Hours: M. to F. 9 – 5
Call for Warehouse times and dates.

office supplies, computers & electronics

REPLAY ELECTRONICS

Another terrific spot for post-Christmas shopping is this electronics store that features new products, close outs and end-of-line brand name goods. Starting December 26, while supplies last, expect additional savings on final clearance items that include Toshiba big screen TVs and DVDs, Kenwood home theatre systems, RCA televisions and much more.

> 1120 The Queensway (just west of Islington Ave.), Toronto.
> Tel: 416-251-9096
> Hours: M to F. 10-6, Sat.10-5, (open on Boxing Day, December 26 ,12-5)

NEW: Replay Electronics

has a new location specializing in custom designed home entertainment systems for those who demand the best quality at an affordable cost.

> 4247 Dundas Street West, Toronto.
> Tel: 416-232-1166

Check out our great selection - it changes constantly!

◀◀**REPLAY**▶▶
E L E C T R O N I C S

■ New Products ■ Close-Outs ■
■ End of Lines ■ Re-Packaged ■
home theatre systems, big screens,
loud speakers, telephones, dvd and vcrs,
subwoofers and hdtv ready television sets.
■ brand name ■ satisfaction guaranteed ■
**1120 THE QUEENSWAY, WEST OF
ISLINGTON 416-251-9096
4247 Dundas St. West
Tel: 416-232-1166**

UPGRADE FACTORY

> 1515 Matheson Blvd. E., Unit B-11 (south of Hwy 401 and east off Dixie Rd.), Mississauga.
> Tel: 905-625-5525
> Web site:www.upgradefactory.ca
> Hours: M. to Sat. 10 – 6

---

office supplies, computers & electronics

STAPLES/BUSINESS DEPOT

Staples/Business Depot is Canada's largest office products superstore chain. With over 7,500 brand name office products, customers will find everything from pens and paper to furniture, business machines and computers, as well as Copy Centre and Business Services. They provide customers with the lowest prices on national brand products, everyday, with associates who really care and provide friendly, knowledgeable service.

Customers can take advantage of three ways to shop: In any one of 200 stores currently across Canada; through the catalogue, and on-line, where they are open for business 24 hours a day, seven days a week. With every order of $50,00 or more (catalogue/on line), they will deliver, free of charge to your home or business address. There are over 60 locations in Ontario to serve your personal or business needs. There are now 200 stores across Canada, including 35 stores in the Greater Toronto Area, and growing.

All locations open 7 days/week, many with extended hours.

Tel: 1-800-668-6888 for individual store hours and a location near you, or access the internet: www.businessdepot.com. www.staples.ca or www.bureauengros.com.

Head Office: 30 Centurian Dr., Markham.
Tel: 905-513-6116

See advertisement on page A25

YOUR FEEDBACK COUNTS

Please tell us about your favourite shopping experiences and those special merchants. where value and quality are their most important products.

You may e-mail ujs at: shoestringshopping@rogers.com or call and leave a message at: 416-236-1489.

---

miscellaneous

- **Resale Goods**
- **A Little Bit of Everything**
- **Malls**
- **Duty Free**

Ransom

resale goods

ARCH INDUSTRIES
Okay grunge-ites, here it is. Before this rag factory turns used jeans into something else, they are offered for sale at $5 a pair, complete with holes, rips and unwashed to boot! Also available are used workwear, coveralls and new fabric. Cash and carry.

   200 Bartor Rd., (west side of Hwy. 400 between Sheppard and Wilson Aves., for Bartor Rd. take Clayson Rd. north off Wilson Ave. or Arrow Rd. north off Sheppard), Toronto.
   Tel: 416 -741-7247
   Hours: M. to F. 7:30 - 5

BEAN SPROUT
   616 Mount Pleasant Rd. (south of Manor Rd.), Toronto.
   Tel: 416-932-3727
   Hours: M. to Sat. 10:30 - 5:30

BEARLY WORN TRADING COMPANY
A great children's consignment shop that carries a good selection of pre-loved children's clothing, toys, books and furniture. They also carry a line of Avent Naturally baby products. You will also find "old fashioned candy" sticks, and wonderful new clothes made by Deborah Keeble, a native of Hillsburgh.

   168B Broadway, turn left at Hwy. #9 West, turn left after third lights, Orangeville.
   Tel: 519-942-5910
   Hours: Tue. Wed. Sat. 10 a.m. to 5 p.m., Thursday an
   Friday 10 a.m. to 6 p.m.

CANADIAN SKI PATROL SKI SWAP 🏢
We are fortunate to have free ski patrolling in Canada - in some countries you have to negotiate a fee before being removed from the mountains after an injury! This huge ski swap is one way that they raise funds to continue their important work. It also presents an excellent way to pick up used equipment. There is a fee into the show but for enthusiasts, the Toronto Ski Show is a must. Ski show is mid-October.

   Exhibition Place on Toronto's waterfront.
   Tel: 416 -745-7511
   Call for exact dates.

resale goods

CASH CONVERTERS
3003 Danforth Rd. Shoppers World Plaza
Tel: 416-693-2274
Call for other locations.

CHIC REPEATS
115 Trafalgar Rd. (near the Lakeshore), Oakville.
Tel: 905-842-0905
Hours: T. to Sat. 10 – 5, Summer hours T. to Sat. 10 – 4

CLARKSBURGERS - RECYCLED CLOTHING AND 'THINGS'
201 Marsh St., (south of the Beaver River bridge on east side-south of
Thornbury), Clarksburg.
Tel: 519- 599-6811
Hours: W. to Sun. 11-5

THE CLASSY ATTIC
1051 Simcoe St. N., Oshawa.
Tel: 905-432-1012
Hours: M. to W. 10 - 5, Thu. 10 -6, F. 10 - 5:30, Sat. 10 - 5

COLLINGWOOD SKI CLUB SKI SWAP 🏠
It's always well done with excellent bargains and always takes place during the
Thanksgiving weekend. You can sell and buy everything from new and used
equipment to clothing. The sale is in October.
Central Base Lodge, Blue Mountain Resorts, seven miles west of
Collingwood on Blue Mountain Rd., Collingwood.
Tel: 705- 445-0231

Abdicate (v.), to give up all hope of ever having a flat stomach.

---

resale goods

COLOURS EXCHANGE

Celebrating its 20th year in business, Colours Exchange is a terrific consignment shop – a favourite for anyone looking for quality in previously owned ladies wear. Great selection of women's designer and high quality clothing, shoes and accessories. Prices are slashed even more during the off-season. Appointments can be arranged to bring in your own items for resale. New arrivals daily.

> 3 Brentwood Rd. N. (One block west of Royal York Rd. north of Bloor St.), Etobicoke.
> Tel: 416-239-0559
> Hours: T.-F. 10-6, Sat. 10 -5:30   See advertisement on page A10

THE COMEBACK 📆

Since 1978, THE COMEBACK has been selling and consigning an extensive variety of ladies and children's clothing and accessories. Racks are filled withy designer and popular labels and include a selection for plus sizes. This is a busy, well-stocked and organized store. Prices are reduced regularly. Two end-of-season sales provide discounts of up to 70% off. Shop now for better selection.

> 4893 Dundas St. W. (south side, west of Islington), Etobicoke.
> Tel: 416-231-0381
> Hours: M. T. W. & Sat. 9:30 - 5, Thu. 9:30 - 8; F. 9:30 - 6
>   See advertisement on page A14

CONTENTS CONNECTION

As the name implies, this quality consignment store offers just about everything you need for your home. Look for furniture, antiques, gifts, collectibles and more......and they have just moved to a much larger location which opened to the public on March 1. Inventory changes often – lots of parking.

> 3321 Bathurst St. (between Lawrence & Wilson Aves.), Toronto.
> Tel: 905-881-6666
> Hours: Open 7 days a week 10-5 (until 8 on W. and Thurs.)

Willy-nilly (adj.), impotent

---

resale goods

DURHAM REGION PARENTS OF MULTIPLE BIRTHS ASSOC. 📷
For the past 15 years, they have hosted a children's clothing & equipment sale. Proceeds go toward a network of support for parents of multiple births. The sales carry gently-used clothing in sizes from newborn to size 14, maternity clothes, baby equipment, toys & crafts. Cash only & no strollers are allowed. March and September Warehouse sales.

> Metro East Trade Centre, Brock Rd., (just north off Hwy. 401), Pickering.
> Tel: 905 - 721-2238

THE ELEGANT GARAGE SALE
> 1588 Bayview Ave., (south of Eglinton Ave.), Toronto.
> Tel:: 416 -322-9744.
> Hours: M. and Tue 11-5, W. and Thur 11-8, F. 11-9, Sat and Sun 11-7

FANTASTIC FLEA MARKET
There are nearly 130 shops at this market, with wide aisles so there is never a crowd. Lots of things for everyone including toys, small appliances, decorations, clothes, used cars, jewellery, tools and much more. This is also where you can pick up a great gift for someone for under $10.

> 2375 Steeles Ave. W. (take Allen Expressway right up to Steeles, turn left one block), North York.
> Tel: 416-306-0032
> Hours: Saturday and Sundays 10 a.m. to 6 p.m.

GOODWILL STORE
This bright, well-organized location has clothing for the whole family as well, everything is colour grouped, with lots of better names and very well priced.

> 382 Queen St. E. (north west corner at Hwy. 410 and Queen St. E.),
> Brampton.
> Tel: 905-453-5252
> Hours: M. to F. 9 - 9, Sat. 9 -6 Sun. 10-5
> Many other locations in Ontario.

HAND ME DOWNS
> 5051 Hwy. 7, Markham.
> Tel: 905-479-1869
> Visit their web page at www.handmedowns.com.
> Hours: Hours vary. Please call for details and other locations.

resale goods

HAPPY HARRY'S
Harry is ready to strip out recyclables & sell the salvaged - everything from kitchen sinks to windows, studs & insulation. His associated company, the Environmental Recycling Group Inc., works not only with homeowners but also as brokers to large de-construction sites, and finding markets for reusable materials to meet provincial recycling regulations. Check out his web page at www.er-group.com! Cash or cheque with ID only.

> 4128 South Service Rd. (east of Walkers Line, north of Harvester Rd.), Burlington.
> Tel:: 905 - 631-0990
> Hours: Call for hours

HomeAGAINdecor
The professionals at L'Elegante, boasting more than 30 years experience in upscale consignments, are introducing HomeAGAINdecor. A practical and alternative means of buying and/or selling finer home décor accessories and furnishings.

> 122 Yorkville Ave., Toronto
> Tel: 416-923-3220
> Hours: M. T. W. & Fri. 10-6, Thu. 10-7, Sat. 9:30-5, Sun. 11-5.
> Sherwood Forest Village, 1900 Dundas St. W., Mississauga.
> Tel: 905-822-9610
> Hours: M. T. W. 10-6, Thu. Fri. 10-7, Sat. 9:30-5, Sun. closed
> See Ad. page 171

See advertisement on page 171

INESRA - I'LL NEVER EVER SHOP RETAIL AGAIN
From unique funky/classic vintage to elegant retro you can splurge without losing your shirt. All items in great condition. Generally $50 and under. Four shows; Spring, Summer, Fall and Winter or by appointment. A Host booking for small groups of 5 or more receive $25 off and complimentary wine and snack.

> 315 Albany Ave., 2nd Floor (E. of Bathurst St. & N. of Dupont Ave., off Bridgeman Ave.), Toronto.
> Tel: 416 -699-5242
> Hours: Call for specific dates and times.

---

resale goods

IT'S WORTH REPEATING
3555 Thickson Rd. N. (north of Rossland Rd. E.), Whitby.
Tel: 905-579-9912
Hours: M. to F. 9:30 - 8, Sat 9:30 - 5, Sun 12 - 5

KIDS KONSIGNMENT
66 Thomas St. Unit 26 (south of Britannia Rd. and between Queen St. and Erin Mills Pkwy.), Streetsville.
Tel: 905-567-7890
Hours: T. & W. 9:30 - 6, Thu. 9:30 - 8, F. 9:30 - 6, Sat. 9 - 5, Sun. 12 - 4
Call for Summer hours

L'ELEGANTE
For more than 30 years, providing the highest quality of upscale resale ladies fashions & service, such as Chanel, Prada, Gucci, and Hermes.
122 Yorkville Ave., Toronto.
Hours: M. T. W. & Fri. 10-6; Thu. 10-7; Sat. 10-6; Sun. 11-5.
Tel: 416-923-3220
Sherwood Forest Village, 1900 Dundas St. W., Mississauga.
Tel: 905-822-9610
Hours: M. T. W. 10-6, Thu. Fri. 10-7, Sat. 9:30-5, Sun. closed

MAGGIE'S CHILDREN'S CONSIGNMENT SHOP
52 Main St. (Hwy #401 west to Mississauga Rd, north to Bush St. in Village of Belfountain, then west to Erin), Erin.
Tel: 519-833-9813.
Hours: T.-F. 10-6, Sat. 10. to 5.

NATIONAL SPORTS EQUIPMENT REPAIR
1540 Lodestar Rd., Unit 5 (west off Dufferin St./Allen Rd, north of Sheppard.), Downsview.
Tel: 416 -638-3408
Hours: M. to F. 8:30 - 5:30

OF THINGS PAST
This huge showroom of consignment furniture has over 18,000 square feet of beautiful pieces which change daily. You'll find many articles of furniture, as well as rugs, lamps, chandeliers and wall hangings. We particularly liked the lovely array of both old and new china pieces. After 60 days, prices are reduced monthly. Their NEW location brings unusual pieces to this exciting venue!
185 Bridgeland Ave. (South of Hwy. #401, west off Dufferin.), Toronto.
Tel: 416-256-9256
Hours: M.-Sat. 10-5.

OFF THE CUFF
5 Broadway Ave. (north of Eglinton Ave., east of Yonge St.), Toronto.
Tel: 416-489-4248
Hours: T. & W. 10 - 6, Thu. 12 - 8, F. 10 - 5 , Sat. 10 - 4
Call for Jan. and Feb. Hours.

ONCE UPON A CHILD
16655 Yonge St., Newmarket.
Tel: 905-715-7939
Hours: M. to F. 10 - 8, Sat. 10 - 6, Sun. 12 - 4
Call for other locations.

resale goods

PHASE 2 CLOTHING INC. - RESALE CLOTHING
260 Lakeshore Rd., Oakville.
Tel: 905-337-0640
Hours: M. to F. 9:30 - 9, Sat. 9:30 - 6, Sun. 12 – 5
Call for other locations

PLAY 'N' WEAR
1722 Avenue Rd. (west side, north of Lawrence Ave.), Toronto.
Tel: 416-782-0211
Hours: T. to Sat. 9:30 - 5, Thu. 9:30 - 8

PLAY IT AGAIN SPORTS - SECOND-HAND SPORTING GOODS
2055 Lawrence Avenue, Scarborough.
(Plus ten other stores in the Greater Toronto area and many more throughout Ontario.)
Tel: 416-285-7529

PRECIOUS SECONDS
A customer friendly store that offers quality, brand-name and designer ladies clothing (2-2 plus), children's clothing (N.B.-teen), maternity wear and a small exclusive men's area. Some new children's items are available at exceptional savings. They also offer books, toys, videos, footwear, equipment, as well as a new giftware section. For shopping moms, there is a safe, secure play area for the children as well. Their motto is "FAMOUS LABELS AT FABULOUS PRICES". Take what you wore YESTERDAY, Sell it TODAY, Buy something new for TOMORROW
14 Oxford St. Richmond Hill.
Tel: 905 - 883-8885
Hours: Mon, Tues, Wed, Fri. 10:00-5:30, Thurs. 10:00-7:00, Sat. 10:00-5:00

PROVIDENCE RETAIL OUTLET
One of our favorites, this 4,700 square foot location is jammed with better brand names, used clothing for the whole family. We spent over an hour and under sixty bucks purchasing a huge bag of clothes. You too will spend lots of time and little money!
152 Main Street, South, Brampton.
Hours: M. to W. 9 - 6, Thu. & F. 10 - 8, Sat. 9 - 6
Tel: 905 - 456-8413

resale goods

THE REPEAT RIDER
1777 Avenue Rd. (south of Wilson Ave.), North York.
Tel: 416-256-5899
Hours: M. to W. & F. 10 - 6, Thu. 10 - 7, Sat. 10 - 5

REPEATS 🔲
With an emphasis on designer labels, Repeats carries a large selection of women's resale clothing. They also have a wide variety of accessories including shoes, handbags and jewellery. They have been in business for over 20 years and have great sales to check out in June and December.
3313 Yonge St. (north of Lawrence Ave.), Toronto.
Tel: 416-481-2325
Hours: M. to Sat. 10 - 6, Sun. 12:30-4:30.

RESTORES -
METROPOLITAN TORONTO HABITAT FOR HUMANITY
Profits are used to build homes for hard-working people who might not otherwise be able to afford a home of their own. The concept of the ReStores is to divert reusable materials from landfill sites - for builders and renovators the incentive is saving on dumping fees as well as paying peanuts for the donated materials. Some locations will also take working appliances, which can provide real savings when compared to new prices. Some locations also take VISA, Interac and of course all take cash. Volunteers are always welcome.
120 North Field Dr. East, (between Davenport Rd. and Bridge St.), Waterloo.
Tel: 519-747-0664
Hours: M. to W. 8:30 - 5, Thu. & F. 9 - 7, Sat. 9 - 3
128 Brock St., Unit 2, (west off Anne St. north of Essa Rd.), Barrie.
Tel: 705-735-2001
Hours: T. to Sat. 9-5:30
18 Coldwater Rd. (E. of Leslie St. between Hwy. 401 & York Mills Rd.), North York.
Tel: 416-510-2223
Hours: M. to F. 10 - 6, Thu. 10 - 9, Sat. 9-3

resale goods

RUGGED REPLAYS
A great consignment store for men that carries everything from jeans to tuxedos. Grade 8 graduation and lots of weddings are just around the corner, so why not look your best for a lot less. For around $100, you'll get a stylish suit, shirt, tie and shoes which sounds almost too good to be true. You will also find lots of new salesman's samples, end of lines and clearances also available here. Visit their web site www.ruggedreplays.com.

> 19 Sawdon Dr., Units 1 & 2 (Hwy. #401, north on Thickson Rd., 3 sets of lights to Burns St. Plaza), Whitby.
> Tel: 905 404-2063
> Hours: M.-W. 10 a.m. to 6 p.m., Thu.-Fri. 10 a.m. to 9 p.m.,
> Sat. 10 a.m. to 5 p.m.

SECOND NATURE BOUTIQUE
Three floors of designer clothing, casual to cocktail, accessories and household items at a fraction of retail. Seventy per cent off on the lower level all the time with merchandise arriving hourly. They have been in business 29 years.

> 514 Mount Pleasant Rd. (at Millwood), Toronto
> Tel: 416 481-4924
> Hours: Monday to Saturday 10 am. to 6 pm
> Website: wwwsecondnaturebtq.com

SHOPPE D'OR LIMITED
> 18 Cumberland St., Toronto.
> Tel: 416-923-2384
> Hours: M. to Sat. 10 - 6

STILL GORGEOUS – WOMEN'S CONSIGNMENT SHOP
> 13065 Hwy. 27, (northeast corner at King Rd.), Nobleton.
> Tel: 905-859-0632.
> Hours: Tues., W. and Sat. 10-4, Thurs. 1-8, F. 10-8.

SWEET REPEATS
> 387 Jane St. (below Annette St.), Toronto.
> Tel: 416-763-0009
> Hours: T. to Sat. 10 - 6

resale goods

THE FASHION GO ROUND
It's an interesting selection of ladies and children's gently used clothing and accessories as well as baby needs, including strollers and playpens.

 6 Brentwood Rd. (south off Bloor St., west of Royal York Rd.), Etobicoke.
 Tel: 416 -236-1220
 Hours: T. to Sat. 10 - 5:30

THINK TWICE 📷
A virtual alphabet for ladies designer label clothing from Armani, DKNY, Escada to Gucci, Guy LaRoche, Lagerfeld and Valentino. Sizes range from 2 to "XL-ent". New sample shoes available, lingerie, bathing suits and accessories. Summer sale through July with a boatload of savings all month.

 1679 Lakeshore Rd. West, (just 5 kms. West of Mississauga Rd.),
 Mississauga.
 Tel: 905-823-2233
 Hours: M.-F. 10-5:30, Sat. 10 - 5   See advertisement on page A20

TORONTO HOCKEY REPAIR LTD.
Not only do they repair equipment, but they sell new and used gear, and manufacture products as well. This location has three floors, offers a discount on new merchandise, and takes trade-ins.

 1592 Bloor St. W. (just east of Keele St.), Toronto.
 Tel: 416-533-1791
 Hours: M. to F. 9 - 7, Sat. 9 - 5, Sun. 11 - 3

TORONTO PARENTS OF MULTIPLE BIRTHS ASSOCIATION - 📷
ANNUAL FALL/WINTER SALE
Friends with twins say this 1-day sale is a great way to shop for used children's clothing, toys, strollers, bedding & equipment. October Warehouse Sale.

 Cedarbrook Community Centre, 91 Eastpark Blvd. (south of Lawrence
 Ave, off Markham Rd.), Scarborough.
 Tel: 416 -760-3944

resale goods

TWICE IS NICE 🏠
Several of our readers frequent this resale store for bargains on ladies and children's clothing, toys and gift items. Inventory is added daily. Consignments are accepted by appointment. Ongoing 50% off sale.

235 Lakeshore Rd. E. (east of Hwy. 10), Port Credit.

Tel: 905-274-5569

Hours: T. to Fri. 11-6, Sat.10-5.

TWICE THE FUN - CHILDREN'S RESALE SHOP
3455 Fairview St. (South of QEW, near Walkers Line) Burlington.

Hours: M.-Thu. & Sat.. 9-6; Fri. 9-8.

TWINS PLUS ASSOCIATION OF BRAMPTON - 🏠
RECYCLING BABY WEAR & GEAR
Expect to find everything in pairs as this non-profit support group holds its bi-annual sale of used baby & children's clothes, toys, books & equipment like double strollers, car seats & high chairs. Sizes are up to size 8. Cash or cheques with I.D. April and October Warehouse Sales.

Locations vary, call for details.

Tel: 905 - 790-1451

WARDROBE EXCHANGE
856 Brock St. N. (north of Hwy. 2), Whitby.

Tel: 905-666-9225

Hours: M. to W. & F. 10 - 5:30, Thu. 10 -7, Sat 10 - 5

WASTEWISE – GIANT GARAGE SALE
Love garage sales? Why not visit Wastewise? They have over 5,000 sq.ft. of bargains just waiting for you. A large selection of good used books, magazines, records and tapes make Wastewise a popular place. They also have adult and children's clothing, small appliances, kitchen items, hardware, knick-knacks, light fixtures, sports equipment, toys, puzzles and games. Donations of antique items are always appreciated for our ongoing silent auction.

36 Armstrong Ave., Georgetown.

Tel: 905-873-8122

Hours: M. to W., F. & Sat. 9 - 5, Thu. 9 - 8

---

resale goods

WHAT IN SAM HILL
101 Main Street, Unit 2 (Hwy 35 to Minden, turn left towards business section), Minden.
Tel: 705-286-2100
Hours: M. to Sat. 10 - 5 Sun. noon to 3

"For those who love the philosophy of hypocrisy and ambiguity."

1. Don't sweat the petty things and don't pet the sweaty things.

2. One tequila, two tequila, three tequila, floor.

3. Atheism is a non-prophet organization.

4. If man evolved from monkeys and apes, why do we still have monkeys and apes?

5. The main reason Santa is so jolly is because he knows where all the bad girls live.

6. I went to a bookstore and asked the saleswoman, "Where's the self-help section?" She said if she told me, it would defeat the purpose.

7. What if there were no hypothetical questions?

8. If a deaf person swears, does his mother wash his hands with soap?

9. If a man is standing in the middle of the forest speaking and there is no woman around to hear him...is he still wrong? [Of course, he is!]

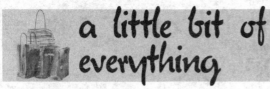
a little bit of everything

BUSY BEE MACHINE TOOLS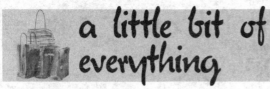
Tel: 416-665-8008
Location: 355 Norfinch Dr., North York
May Garage Sale. Call for dates and hours.

CANADA SALVAGE COMPANY
505 The Queensway E., Unit 5 (one block west of Cawthra Rd. at Tedlo St.), Mississauga.
Tel: 905-897-7800
Hours: M. to F. 9 - 5

CENTURY SERVICES
Locations and hours vary so please call for details.
Tel: 416-495-8338

CIGAR STUDIO
To make way for the arrival of spring goods, they are having a St. Valentine's sale massacre. All Eric Nording pipes are 35% off, all 2001 pipes of the year are 40% off and premium pipe tins are 15% off. Three humidor styles are on sale, the F800 model is $199 reg. $329. Cigar jars also are 50% off for this sale. No better time to pick up gifts of cigar cutters, cases and lighters at 40% off. If you thought you could never afford a St Dupont lighter, check out this sale.
4 Willingdon Blvd., (just north of Bloor St. east of Royal York Rd.), Toronto.
Tel: 416-237-9470.
Hours: Call for sale dates: Monday to Wednesday 10 a.m. to 7 p.m., Thursday and Friday 10 a.m. to 8 p.m., Saturday 10 a.m. to 6 p.m. and Sunday noon to 5

CITY OF TORONTO DEPT. OF PURCHASING AND SUPPLY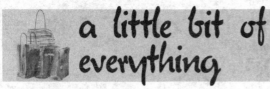
This semi-annual event earns money for the municipal government by finding new homes for office equipment and furnishings, vehicles, motorcycles, construction equipment, industrial and consumer goods and lawn and garden supplies no longer needed by the City of Toronto. Please call the hotline number below for sale dates. T.B.A. Warehouse Sale.
Metro Transportation Yard, 64 Murray Rd. (west of Dufferin St. and north off Wilson Ave.), Downsview.
Tel: 416-392-1991 (HOT-LINE)

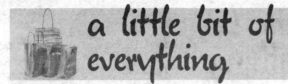
a little bit of everything

COLT-PAK CONTAINERS

If you are moving soon we have found a great packaging warehouse. They offer fabulous deals on moving cartons from $2.00, wardrobe containers, tape, bubble wrap, newsprint or just about anything that is needed to handle a move.

151 Sterling Rd (2 blocks west of Lansdowne, north side of Dundas St.) Toronto.

Tel: 416-535-7234.

Hours: Monday to Friday 9 a.m. to 5 p.m.

CONSOLIDATED SALVAGE - INSURANCE SALVORS

Their stock changes frequently so it's a good idea to return regularly. Cash only.

2446 Cawthra Rd. (north of Queensway), Mississauga.

Tel: 905-276-4230

Hours: M. to F. 9 - 4:30 After labor day they will be open on Saturdays from 9 – 3

COSTCO WHOLESALE

Costco is a member organization, charging shoppers an annual fee to help defray operating expenses, which contributes to a lower cost base and lower overall prices. We have found that this "Big Box" store does live up to its advertised "First Quality, Low Warehouse Prices!" slogan. From computers and electronics, to cleaning supplies to fresh salmon and baked goods, if they have what you need when you visit their well-located stores, you won't be disappointed. They do tend to package food and household supplies in large quantities for families, but in most cases savings are significant. They have an excellent, no hassle refund/exchange policy on goods purchased. Payment by American Express, Interac, cheque or cash only.

Several locations in the Greater Toronto Area and larger cities across Canada and the US.

Open seven days/week. Check your Tel: directory or www.costco.com for the location nearest you.

CRAZY DAVE'S - LIQUIDATION OUTLET

Varies according to sales.

Tel: 905-609-8233

Hours: Call for location and hours.

a little bit of everything

CROWN ASSETS - DISTRIBUTION CENTRE
One of our readers tipped us off to this government retail store, serving as a depot for items Canada Post is unable to deliver. CD's, books, tapes, cosmetics & sundry articles that haven't made it to their final destinations, end up here. Prices are low, but goods can look pretty beat up and tired. Public sales of vehicles & equipment are held once a month also.

6205 Kestrel Rd. (north of Hwy 401 in the Britannia & Tomken Rds. area), Mississauga.
Tel: 416-973-6300
Hours: T. & Thu. 10 - 3

DANBURY SALES
25 Civic Rd., (south of Eglinton Ave. E., east off Warden Ave. and just north of the huge water tower), Scarborough.
Tel: 416-630-5241
Hours: M. to F. 10 - 8, Sat. 10 - 5, Sun. 12 – 5

EMPIRE AUCTIONS
Once a month Empire Auctions offers, with no minimum and no reserve, a wide selection of furniture, estate and modern jewellery, collectibles and hand-woven Persian rugs. You'll find prices far below retail. Sales every four weeks – call for dates.

165 Tycos Dr. (south of Lawrence Ave. and west off Dufferin St.), Toronto.
Tel: 416-784-4261
Website: www.empireauctions.com

Lymph (v.), to walk with a lisp.

---

a little bit of everything

HADASSAH-WIZO BAZAAR 🛍
Another Toronto institution is this annual event. This year marks their 78th anniversary, and as always there will be bargains for the whole family. Visit the Auction Centre and bid on fabulous items. Great food, fabulous fashions, household treasures and lots of gently used and new items. Admission is only a "toonie" and children under 5 are free. Proceeds go to medical care.

    The Better Living Centre, Exhibition Place, Toronto
Tel: 416-630-8373 (To confirm date)
E-Mail: www.canadian-hadassah-wizo.org
Hours: Wednesday, October 25, 9:00 a.m. - 8:00 p.m.

KABOOM FIREWORKS
    Outlet store at 202 Laird Dr. (south of Eglinton Ave.), Toronto.
Tel: 416-467-9111

LIQUIDATION SALES BY IMPORTERS CLEARANCE CENTRE 🛍
    Call for location.
Tel: 905-470-7708

LOBLAWS/SUPERCENTRE PHARMACIES/ - INDEPENDENT GROCERS
Loblaws is not allowed to publicize its prescription dispensing fees but thank goodness a reader told us so WE can! There are several area Loblaws or Supercentres with some of the lowest prices on prescriptions in the province. With over 87 stores in Ontario, please call the location nearest you.

M.S. HALPERN AND SON - BARGAIN WAREHOUSE
    2420 Finch Ave. West, Units 21-22 (west of Weston Rd., behind the Sunoco Station), Toronto
Tel: 416-740-1696
Hours: Thu. & F. 9 - 3, Sat. 9 - 12

Gargoyle (n.), an olive-flavored mouthwash.

---

a little bit of everything

MEAFORD FACTORY OUTLET

We found this large outlet after skiing and spent lots of time checking out all the deals. February is their "Sweetheart Event" with special pricing for the month on tools, giftware, furniture, clothing, office supplies, linen, etc. Mattresses and box spring sets are priced from $88. Receive a case of Orbitz pop free with every $20 purchase.

   278 Cook St. Meaford,
   (Just off Hwy. 26, follow the signs).
   Tel: 519-538-4443
   Hours: M.-Th. - 10-6; Fri 10 -9; Sat. 10 -6; Sun. 11 –5

METRO EAST TRADE CENTRE

Featuring a number of retailers gathered under one roof for convenient discount shopping. Great prices from Holt Renfrew, Corning, Cambridge Towel, Royal Doulton, Moulinex and several others. Expect to find clearances on footwear from Bata and Athletes World, with great names like Nike, Reebok, Converse and others. Sales throughout the year include Tip Top, Cambridge Towel, Procter and Gamble, Black & Decker, and Jones Apparel Group. Brand names may vary from sale to sale but they are always well known names. Warehouse sales happen periodically - call for info or to add your name to their mailing list. Parking and admission free. Wheelchair accessible.

   1899 Brock Road, Pickering
   Hours: M. to F. 9-5. Call for weekend and warehouse sale hours.
   Tel: For Warehouse information and sale dates call 905 - 427-0744.

ROBINSON'S GENERAL STORE, DORSET

   One Main St., Dorset
   Open 7 days/week, year round.
   Tel: 705-766-2415.

Balderdash (n.), a rapidly receding hairline.

---

a little bit of everything

THE SHOPPING CHANNEL CLEARANCE OUTLET

Now you can shop the Shopping Channel (tSc) in person at their first OffAir Outlet store. This new 15,000 square foot store is stocked with their most popular televised and clearance products. Discount levels increase each month the products remain in the store. Doorcrasher specials include products from Jerome Alexander, Joan Rivers, the Art Gallery of Ontario and more.

100A Orfus Road (west off Dufferin Street, south of the 401), Toronto.
Tel: 416-783-3961
or visit their web site:www.tSc.ca
Hours: Sun. to W., 10-6, Thurs. and F. 10-9, Sat. 10-6.

STRAWBERRY FESTIVAL

On the last Saturday in June, you'll find Main Street, Stouffville closed to host a wide variety of Strawberry Festival activities. Main Street merchants will offer a variety of bargains, and local artisans will be on hand with unique items. A terrific street sale and close to 80 vendors on hand make it a fun shopping experience in a country village. Of course you'll find strawberries everywhere for both picking and eating!

Main Street, (9th line and Stouffville Road), Stouffville.
Tel: 905-640-0749
Hours: Parade at 9:15 a.m., vendors and street entertainment until evening.

USAVE

We know our male readers will love this warehouse. It's jammed with lots of tools, hardware, plumbing supplies, electronics and more at 50 - 75% off. One of our readers (Alan) alerted us to this great find as he had just bought one of the new Razor scooters here for $99 that is sold elsewhere for $129. We even found cellular accessories at great prices. If you love tools like our guys do, this is definitely worth a visit.

4610 Dufferin Street, Unit 21B (three streets north of Finch Ave.), Toronto.
Tel: 416-665-5500
Hours: M. to Fri. 10:00 – 5, Sat. noon - 4:00, Closed Sunday.

a little bit of everything

VICTORY FIREWORKS

From simple sparklers to exotic pyrotechniques, you'll find everything here at excellent prices. We found several unusual items we'd never seen anywhere else. A dazzling selection available through this outlet year round and they always increase their hours around holiday weekends. Free delivery on orders over $150.00 and on orders over $300.00 anywhere in Canada.

19 Harlech Crt. (Bayview Ave. and John St. area).
Thornhill.
Tel: 905-771-0169.
Web site: www.victoryfireworks.com.
Hours: Call for store hours.

YOU'RE THE GROOMER

8100 Yonge Street, Unit 7, Thornhill.
Tel: 905-886-8353
Web site: www.yourethegroomer.com
Hours: Tue, Wed. & Fri. 9 to 6., Thu. 9 to 9, and Sat. 9 to 5

More Philosophical Thinking

11. Is there another word for synonym?

12. Isn't it a bit unnerving that doctors call what they do "practice"?

13. Where do forest rangers go to "get away from it all?"

14. What do you do when you see an endangered animal eating an endangered plant?

15. If a parsley farmer is sued, can they garnish his wages?

16. Would a fly without wings be called a walk?

17. Why do they lock gas station bathrooms?? Are they afraid someone will clean them?

 malls

CANADA ONE FACTORY OUTLETS

Experience the best in name brand outlet shopping in Niagara Falls, Ontario at Canada One. Located just five minutes from the Falls, Canada One Factory Outlets offers you great brand names with even greater prices.

This upscale manufacturers factory outlet mall includes Battery Plus, Black & Decker, The Body Shop Depot, Cambridge Towels, Claire's Accessories, Club Monaco, Danier Leather, Escada, Esprit, Guess, InWear, Jayset, Kodiak, La View En Rose, Levi's, Liz Clairborne, Mexx, Ninke, Nine West, Oromart Jewellery, Parasuco Jeans, Phantom, Polo Jeans Co., Polo Ralph Lauren, Reebok, Rockport, Rocky Mountain Chocolate Factory, Roots, Samsonite, Time Factory Watch Outlet, Tommy Hilfiger, Tootsies, Tristan & AMERICA, Urban Behavior & Villerooy & Boch. Take a break from shopping and visit their food court area with Asian Gourmet, Burger King or Cupps Coffee House. Special incentives for all group arrivals with plenty of motorcoach parking.

> 7500 Lundy's Lane (at the QEW). Plenty of parking and wheelchair accessible.
>
> Hours: 363 days per year (closed Christmas Day and New Years Day) M-Sat. 10 to 9. Sun. and Holidays 10 to 6. Sat. (January 1-April 30) 10 to 6.
> Tel: 905-356-8989. (Call for additional information)
> Web site www.canadaoneoutlets.com.

See advertisement on inside front cover

FACTORY OUTLET COMPLEX

This industrial-style complex with four outlets is situated toward the south end of Hamilton and close to the Q.E.W. Included here is Len's Mill Store, a large factory outlet that provides bargains on everything from work wear to fabrics, craft supplies to clothing for the entire family. The Arrow Shirt store has a wide selection of first and second quality men's clothing as well as some women's wear.

> 41 Brockley Dr.(Centennial Pkwy., South from the Q.E.W., Brockley is East of the Pkwy. Off Barton St. E.), Hamilton.
> Len's Mill:
> Hours: M. to Sat. 10. - 5, Thu. & F. to 9, Sun. 12:30 - 4:30
> Tel: 905 - 560-5367
> Arrow:
> Hours: M. to Sat. 9 - 5, F. to 9, Sun. noon - 4
> Tel: 905 - 578-0055

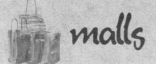 malls

COOKSTOWN MANUFACTURER'S OUTLET

Cookstown is bigger and better than ever and a great place to stop on the way to cottage country. Their recent expansion opened this spring with some great new stores, bringing the count to over 50 direct outlets. Tommy Hilfiger has a huge store stocked with first quality men's, women's and children's wear, all substantially reduced. Polo Jeans offers quality products created for the modern and spirited with high style. At Campus Crew believe it or not, there is nothing over $20. They have a huge selection of styles for men and women. Big savings also at the Calvin Klein Outlet in everything from flares and halter tops to t's and boxers for everyone. Tiger Brand, manufacturer of Non-Fiction has also opened with 100% cotton fleece at bargain prices for the whole family. While you shop, there is mini-golf and playgrounds for the children. Additional stores include:

Animale Outlet
Liz Clairborne Outlet
The Baby's Room Warehouse
The Bag Factory
Beardmore Leathers Factory Outlet
Black & Decker Factory Store
Bookco
Bricks & Blocks – Lego Outlet
Bridges Home Decor
Cadbury Factory Store
Calvin Klein Outlet
Cambridge Towel & Bedding Outlet
Campus Crew Outlet
Card & Paper Place
Corning Revere Factory Store
Dansk Factory Store
Einstein's Laminated Art
Greg Norman Outlet
Herbert's Outlet Post
Home Essentials Outlet/Philips Factory Store
Jack Rabbit's Clothing Co.

Jones Factory Finale
Kodiak Factory Outlet
Levi's Outlet
Mattel Factory Outlet
Modrobes Outlet
New York Clothing Company
Nike Factory Store
Nine West Shoe Studio
Olde Tyme Kettle Kitchen
Olsen Collection Outlet
Oromart
Paderno Cookware Factory Store
Paz Fashions
Polo Jean Outlet
Radio Shack Outlet
Reebok Factory Direct
Rockport Factory Direct
Rogers AT&T Wireless Express
Royal Doulton Outlet
Samsonite Company Store
Sunglass Plus
The Silver Dollar

See advertisement on page A28

malls

The Sock Factory
The Time Factory - By Timex Umbro
Factory Outlet
Tiger Brand Knitting Outlet
Tommy Hilfiger Company Store
Tootsies Factory Shoe Market
Umbro Factory Outlet Inc.
Villeroy & Bock Factory Store

Warnaco Factory Outlet
Plus Food Services INCLUDE:
Coffee Time
Harvey's/Swiss Chalet
Pizza Mondo
The Sandwich Outlet
Teriaki Wok

About 35 minutes north of Metro. Take Highway 400 to Highway 89 and look for the water tower (southeast corner), Cookstown.
Tel: 705- 458-1371
www.cookstownoutletmall.net for more information.
Hours: M. to F. 10 - 9, Sat., Sun. & holidays 9 - 6, except Christmas, New Year's Day.
See advertisement on page A28

DIXIE OUTLET MALL

One of Canada's biggest and best one stop shopping destinations, has over 100 brand names stores, at low outlet prices. When you are hunting for great deals, you don't have to search far and wide, you can find all your favourite brand names for less here.   There is a wide array of new outlet stores as well as your favourites such as Addition-Elle, Au Coton Depot, Jacob, Jay Set Outlet, Tabi International, Warner's Outlet, Hy & Zel's Drug Warehouse, Michaels, Sears Clearance Outlet and Winners.   There are great footwear fashions stores here such as Aldo for Less, Ali Baba Shoe Outlet, Bata Shoe Outlet, Budget Shoe Warehouse, Payless Shoesource, and The Shoe Company. For men they have International Clothiers, Marvellous Maax and Tip Top Warehouse Outlet. Something here for everyone such as Buffalo Jeans Outlet, Jean Machine, Northern Reflections Outlet, Stitches, UB Fashion Outlet, Accessories Club, Claire's Accessories, Cosmetics N'More for Less Factory Outlet, Vivah, Academy Athletic Wear, Footlocker, Benix, The Bombay Company Outlet, Brands for Less, Canadian Hardware, Home Furnishings Factory Outlet, Stokes and three great specialty discount stores, A Buck or Two, The Incredible Five and Ten and 10 of Canada.. Their specialty services include Bell World Outlet Centre, K. Edward Cigar & News, Key Man Engravables, Sew Right. We Make It Fit, Photo Imaging Outlet, and Queen Elizabeth Flowers. New to the mall is a No Frills grocery store. Ample free parking, lockers, lost and found, food court, stroller rentals, complimentary

---

malls

wheelchairs, non-resident tax refund forms and spacious restrooms are some customer conveniences.

1250 South Service Road, Dixie south of the QEW in Mississauga.

Tel: For further information call 905-278-3494.

Hours: M.-F. 10 - 9; Sat. 9:30 - 6; Sun. noon – 6

See advertisement on page A5

HEARTLAND TOWN CENTRE

Bounded by Mavis and McLaughlan Rds. and Britannia Rd. W. and Matheson Blvd., Besides the usual 'big box' stores you will find the following outlets:

Cotton Ginny Outlet Store:

Tel: 905 - 648-9868.

Roots Canada:

Tel: 905 - 501-1200.

Danier:

Tel: 905 - 501-1333.

Harry Rosen Menswear Outlet Store:

Tel: 905 - 890-3100.

OTTAWA STREET

Dozens of stores & outlets, many focusing on textile bargains, are worth investigating, especially if you sew. We visited several fabric stores & others selling everything from candles & wrap to bath sets, silverware & even rubber dinosaur stamps at excellent prices. There are craft supplies & yarns - it's a treasure trove, but be prepared to spend time hunting for bargains.

Ottawa St. (between Kenilworth and Gage Aves. Go south off Barton St. E.), Hamilton.

SOUTHWORKS OUTLET MALL

Wander through this converted 150 year old foundry, you will be stepping back into history as you walk around more than 140,000 square feet of magnificent old limestone buildings. Browse our stores where brand names like Corning, Florsheim Shoes, Jones New York, Revlon, Black & Decker, Cambridge Towel, Far West, Kodiak, Timberland and Nine West are marked way under regular mall prices! Southworks Antiques has 30,000 sq. feet of antiques and collectibles to make your shopping visit a great experience. Tuesdays are for Seniors. Have Fun! Find Bargains! www.southworks.ca

The Shops at Southworks Outlet Mall: (All numbers are in the 519 area)

A Touch of Nature-622-9452

See advertisement on page A29

 malls

Animale Women's Fashions-622 7888
Black & Decker-624-8824
Bookworks of Cambridge-623 7531
Cambridge Custom Brew 624-0791
Cambridge Towel & Bedding 622-5542
Corning Factory Store 624-9911
Cosmetics N'More for Less 620-2625
Down Under Wear 624-1522
Endlines 740-1522
Florshiem Shoes 621-7211
The Flower Market 740-1802
The Golf Ball Store 624-1331
Kodiak 623-0037
Island Beach Co 621-2860
JACKS Coffee Co. 624-1922
Jack Rabbits Clothing Co. 622-6111
Jones Factory Finale 740-3777
Just Because 624-0860
Lakeland Trading Co. 623-5819
Oromart 624-8540
Paderno Cookware 623-8652
Shoes 22 740-8093
The Sock Factory 623-3069
Travellers Warehouse Ltd. 622-5232
    64 Grand Avenue South, Cambridge.
    Tel: 519-740-0380
    Hours: M. T. and Wed. 9:30 - 6, Thu. & Fri. 9:30 - 8, Sat. 9 - 6., Sun 11 - 5
See advertisement on page A29

ST. JACOBS FACTORY OUTLET MALL

Many of you who like planning a day outing will want to plan a visit to this outlet mall - especially now that Phase Three is complete and the Cambridge Towel & Bedding Mill Outlet store has now opened with 10,000 square feet of savings on accessories for bedroom, bath and kitchen.

Brooks, Cadbury Factory Store, Cambridge Towell, Cosmetics 'N More For Less, Cotton Wave, Country Blue, Country Gentleman Barber, Countryside Toy Outlet (LEGO). Country Linens and More, Einstein's Laminated Art, Farm Pantry, Florsheim Factory Outlet, Jack Rabbit's Children's Clothing, Jones Factory Finale, Kodiak Outlet, Levi's Outlet, Liz Claiborne Factory Outlet,

malls

Mattel Factory Outlet, McGrillicuddy's, Olde Tyme Kettle Kitchen, Oromart, Paderno Cookware, Laran Leather, Red Coral, Reebok, Royal Doulton, Scooter's Café, Sock Factory, Spotlight Kids Wear, Time Factory Watch Outlet, Toy Planet (Hasbro) Tootsies Factory Shoe Market, Travellers Warehouse, Villeroy & Boch, Warner's Intimate Apparel, Wicks 'N Wax, World kitchen
> From Hwy 401 take Hwy 8 west to Kitchener, Waterloo, then ramp to Hwy 86 Waterloo, to Road 15, left to Farmer's Market Road
> Open daily including most holidays. M. to F. 9:30 - 9, Sat. 8:30 - 6, Sun. 12-5.
> Tel:: 1-800-265-3353 or
> Web Site: www.stjacobs.com.
> See advertisement on page A27

THORNHILL SQUARE - SHOPPING CENTRE
Stores at this location include Phantom Outlet, 905 - 889-2135, for brand-name hosiery, tights, socks, swimsuits and exercise wear, Cotton Ginny, 905 - 889-7005, for casual cotton ladies wear, and Dreams Downy Duvet, 905 - 707-0887, for down duvets, pillows and linens. Also included is The Shoe Company 905 - 886-3997, Winners 905 - 731-3201 and their newest addition, Books for Less 905 - 763-1543.
> John St. at Bayview Ave. (between Steeles Ave. & Hwy. 7), Thornhill.
> Hours: Mall hours M. to F. 10 - 9, Sat. 9:30 - 6, Sun. 12 - 5
> Tel: 905 - 886-2595

WARDEN POWER CENTRE 🛒
Lots of new looks and new stores at this outlet centre means its probably time to drop in and see what's new for yourself. New to the Centre is and Thyme Maternity. The stores offers a wide selection of clothing lines that include Liz Golf, Liz and Company, Liz Sport, and more in a full range of sizes. Items are at least 30% off, with some as high as 50-70%. Thyme Maternity knows that pregnant women want to look stylish and trendy but still be comfortable at a great price - which they do at prices that are up to 50% off regular retail.
Laura Shoppes is now a permanent store carrying a full line of professional women's wear, Warner's has moved to larger premises with a wider variety of

See advertisement on outside back cover

malls

women's lingerie, and Laura Secord has newly renovated their store and now even carries ice cream. Black and Decker has also moved into new space and offers a wide range of small appliances and outdoor items at 20% off regular retail. All items come with a 30 day guarantee.

    Warden Avenue, just north of St. Clair Ave., Toronto.

    Hours: M to Fri 10-9, Sat 9:30 - 6, Sun 12-5

    Tel:: 416 -752-8366

See advertisement on outside back cover

WINDSOR CROSSING PREMIUM OUTLETS

Only a few of hours drive from Toronto and you can shop at one of Canada's newest outlet centers. They have premium brand name outlet stores such as Adidas, Ecco Shoes, Danier Leather, Nike, Tommy Hilfiger, Guess, Reebok, Polo Jeans Co. and so much more. They offer a large selection of men's, ladies and children's clothing, sportswear, athletic gear, and home accessories. From now to September 17th they are having a back-to-school contest and you could win a $500 shopping spree or one of 30 back packs loaded with school supplies, and much more. You'll find savings of up to 70% off everyday.

    1555 Talbot Road, Windsor. Take Hwy. #401 west to exit 3A and follow signs to Ambassador Bridge; located at the intersection of Hwy. #3 and Sandwich West Parkway.

    Tel: 519-972-7111 or toll free 1-866-613-5172.

    Hours: Open 7 days a week, M. to Fri. 10 a.m. to 9 p.m., Sat. & Sun. 10 a.m. to 6

> ### Parasites - What you see from the top of the Eiffel Tower.

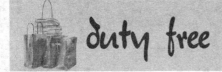

PEACE BRIDGE DUTY FREE

Most of us don't even realize what terrific bargains there can be at a duty free shop - and this one is the largest in North America. It's not just a shop - they also have a travel service center, a food court and a business centre. Merchandise areas include men's and women's clothing from top designers at an average savings of 25%, fragrances and cosmetics, sunglasses and watches (which average 30% less than retail), china and crystal, and of course alcohol. Any questions on allowances can be directed to the helpful staff who are well versed with the regulations. Next time you travel into the United States don't forget to take advantage of your right to shop duty free.

Last exit before the Peace Bridge as you head towards Buffalo at the inter section of the QEW and Central Avenue, Ft. Erie.
Wheelchair accessible.
Toll free: 1 - 800 - 361-1302.
Hours: Open 365 days/year, 24 hours/day.

WORLD DUTY FREE AMERICAS

If your summer travel plans includes a trip to the US, you really should drop into one of these duty free shops before returning to Canada. Choose from a wide selection of top brand names at prices that, even with our exchange, adds up to large savings. Save up to 50% on premium spirits, wine and beer, as well as tobacco. Designer fragrances, watches and crystal are also available. Other services include currency exchange, restrooms and free coffee - of course you must stay within the allowable government guidelines when returning to Canada, but their staff can help if you have any questions.

Peace Bridge Plaza (I-90 to I-190, exit at Peace Bridge Plaza,
Buffalo, NY .
Tel: 716-886-5000
Rainbow Bridge Plaza, Niagara Falls, NY
Tel: 716-284-9736
Open 7 days/week, 8:00 a.m. - 9:00 p.m. (11:00 p.m. during the summer)

Testicle (n.), a humorous question in an exam.

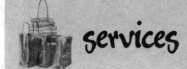services

ARORA
This company operates a service location that offers great value on new and refurbished small electrical appliances and personal care products. All products come with a full warranty at prices that are 30 to 50% lower than retail.
488 Bloor St. W. (one block east of Bathurst Street), Toronto.
Tel: 416-532-8544
Hours: Monday to Friday 10 a.m. to 7 p.m., Saturday 10 a.m. to 6 p.m., Sunday noon to 5 p.m.

FANTASTIC SAMS
We heard about this hair salon through a friend who was looking for a good hair stylist at a reasonable price. Of course we had to go and check it out for ourselves. Prices are excellent, service is friendly, and we were both very impressed by both the cut and the colour treatment at a total price of $45.95. Great spot for the whole family.
2625B Weston Road (Crossroads Centre), Toronto
Tel: 416-243-5088
Hours: Monday, Tuesday and Wednesday 9:00 a.m. to 8:00 p.m., Thursday and Friday 9:00 a.m. to 9:00 p.m., Saturday 9:00 a.m. to 6:00 p.m., Sunday 11:00 a.m. to 5:00 p.m.
See advertisement on page A16

ONE NINETY NINE DRY CLEANING
Doing a winter clean out? We found wholesale dry cleaners with excellent prices to help you out with this job. They have some of the lowest prices on dry cleaning we have seen around, partly due to their state of the art computerized equipment. Regular cleaning items such as pants, suit jackets, sweaters and blouses are $2.99 a piece and coats start at $3.99 with two-day service. One-hour service is available by request.
354 Supertest Rd., (north of Finch, west off Dufferin St.), Downsview.
Tel: 416-663-8247.
Hours: Mon. to Fri. 7 to 5, Sat. 9-5.

See advertisement on page A6

warehouse sale

...monthly calender

These dates were available at time of publication. For those not listed, or TBA (to be announced at later date), call for information and visit the weekly Shoestring Shopping Guide column in The Toronto Star.

january

warehouse sale

COLOURS EXCHANGE
DANYA
COSMETIC WAREHOUSE SALE
IMAGES THAT SUIT
LINEA INTIMA
KORRY'S CLOTHIERS
RITCHIE COUTURE BRIDAL SALE
SPORTS WORLD

february

warehouse sale

BARDEAUS FAMILY FASHIONS AND
   SPORTING GOODS CENTRE
IMAGES THAT SUIT
NORMA PETERSON FASHIONS

march

warehouse sale

ART IN IRON
BLACK AND DECKER
DAREE IMPORTS AND SALES INC.
BARDEAUS FAMILY FASHIONS AND
   SPORTING GOODS CENTRE
DURHAM REGION PARENTS OF
   MULTIPLE BIRTHS ASSOC.
HOLT RENFREW LAST CALL
MR. B'S "FAMOUS" WAREHOUSE SALE
TORONTO PARENTS OF MULTIPLE BIRTHS
SPORTS WORLD

april

warehouse sale

CAMCO MAJOR APPLIANCE SALE
GIFT-PAK
GREENHAWK HARNESS AND
   EQUESTRIAN SUPPLIES
JOBSON AND SONS LTD.
LISA'S COSMETICS
MILLENIUM
PARKHURST - WAREHOUSE SALE
PHANTOM INDUSTRIES WAREHOUSE SALE
SNUG AS A BUG
SUNGLASS SAFARI
RAN'S MATERNITY WAREHOUSE SALE
TOM'S PLACE SPRING WAREHOUSE SALE
TWINS PLUS ASSOCIATION OF BRAMPTON
RECYCLING BABY WEAR & GEAR

may

warehouse sale

ACCESSORY CONCEPTS
BATH N' BEDTIME
BELVEDERE
BUSY BEE MACHINE TOOLS
DANBY PRODUCTS
DANSK WAREHOUSE SALE
DOWN UNDER LINENS -
  WAREHOUSE OUTLET
GARBO GROUP
JORDI INTERNATIONAL FABRICS
MARY MAXIM TENT SALE
MIKASA
MR. B'S "FAMOUS" WAREHOUSE SALE
NORTH YORK PRO SHOP SALE
JOBSON AND SONS LTD.
REPEATS
STYLE KRAFT SPORTSWEAR
SUPER ELECTRIC WAREHOUSE SALE

june

warehouse sale

CONCORD CANDLE TENT SALE
DANSK WAREHOUSE SALE
FREDA'S
GEORGE BOND SPORTS
JOBSON AND SONS LTD.
NORAMA DESIGN WAREHOUSE SALE
REPEATS
ROYAL SHIRT COMPANY
STOUFFVILLE STYRAWBERRY FESTIVAL
SUPER ELECTRIC

july

warehouse sale

FASHION ACCESSORIES - WAREHOUSE OUTLET
GRANNY TAUGHT US HOW
IMAGES THAT SUIT
LA CACHE OUTLET SALE
LE FIRME
LINEA INTIMA
MR. B'S "FAMOUS" WAREHOUSE SALE
THE WEATHERVANE
THINK TWICE

august

warehouse sale

BARDEAUS FAMILY FASHIONS AND
  SPORTING GOODS CENTRE
DISCOUNT INTGERIOR DESIGN
JUSTWHITESHIRTS.COM
NORMA PETERSON FASHIONS
PARKHURST - WAREHOUSE SALE
THE BOMBAY COMPANY OUTLET STORE

september

warehouse sale

BARDEAUS FAMILY FASHIONS AND
  SPORTING GOODS CENTRE
BELVEDERE
DISCOUNT INTERIOR DESIGN WAREHOUSE
DURHAM PARENTS OF MULTIPLE BIRTHS
EDDIE BAUER
EUROPE BOUND
GIFT IDEAZ
MARKHAM VITAMIN WAREHOUSE OUTLET
MR. B'S "FAMOUS" WAREHOUSE SALE
TRINITY COLLEGE BOOK SALE
SPORTS WORLD

october

warehouse sale

ALDERBROOK FALL/WINTER SALE
AURORA COLLECTIBLE FINE CHINA & CRYSTAL
CANADIAN SKI PATROL SKI SWAP
COLLINGWOOD SKI CLUB SKI SWAP
EXECUTIVE FURNITURE RENTALS
FREEMAN FORMAL WEAR - WAREHOUSE SALE
GREENHAWK HARNESS AND EQUESTRIAN
HADASSAH-WIZO BAZAAR
JOBSON AND SONS LTD.
JORDI INTERNATIONAL FABRICS
MR. B'S "FAMOUS" WAREHOUSE SALE
PRECIDIO
RIZCO TOY & GIFT WAREHOUSE SALE
TORONTO PARENTS OF
  MULTIPLE BIRTHS ASSOCIATION
TWINS PLUS ASSOCIATION OF BRAMPTON
RECYCLING BABY WEAR & GEAR
TUXEDO ROYALE
RAN'S MATERNITY WAREHOUSE SALE
WILLIAM ASHLEY WAREHOUSE SALE

PHANTOM INDUSTRIES WAREHOUSE SALE
RAN'S MATERNITY
RIZCO TOY & GIFT WAREHOUSE SALE
THE WEATHERVANE
TILLEY ENDURABLES
WILLIAM ASHLEY WAREHOUSE SALE

december

warehouse sale

ACCESSORY CONCEPTS
ASH CITY
CANALITE
COLONIAL JEWELLERY
DOWNTOWN DUVET
EBC GIFTS AND COLECTIBLES
JUSTWHITESHIRTS.COM
LISA'S COSMETICS WAREHOUSE SALE
MR. B'S "FAMOUS" WAREHOUSE SALE
PEPPERTREE KLASSICS
PLEASANT PHEASANT
QSP/READER'S DIGEST WAREHOUSE SALE
REPEATS
REVLON WAREHOUSE SALE
RIZCO TOY & GIFT WAREHOUSE SALE
ROYAL SHIRT CO.
THE UMBRA FACTORY SALE
THE WEATHERVANE
TILLEY CHRISTMAS SALE

november

warehouse sale

AURORA COLLECTIBLE FINE CHINA & CRYSTAL
BANFF DESIGNS
BATH N' BEDTIME
BELVEDERE INTERNATIONAL
DANSK WAREHOUSE SALE
DOWN UNDER LINENS - WAREHOUSE OUTLET
FASHION ACCESSORIES - WAREHOUSE OUTLET
GANZ
GARBO GROUP
GEORGE BOND SPORTS
GIFT-PAK/DAREE IMPORTS AND SALES LTD.
GRANNY TAUGHT US HOW
HERITAGE INTERIORS
JOBSON AND SONS LTD.
LISA'S COSMETICS
MILLENIUM
MUSKOKA LAKES
PARKHURST - WAREHOUSE SALE

to be announced

T.B.A. warehouse sale

ACCESSORY CONCEPTS INC.
ACTION INVENTORY COSMETIC WAREHOUSE
SALE
ARTEBRA GIFTS AND IMPORTS WAREHOUSE
SALE
AVONLEA TRADITIONS INC. WAREHOUSE SALE
AYUS OUTLET SALE
BARRYMORE FURNITURE MANUFACTURER
BROOKS WAREHOUSE SALE
BRUZER SPORTS GEAR FACTORY SALE
CANADA STAINED GLASS SECONDS SALE
CHRISTIAN DAVID
CITY OF TORONTO DEPT. OF PURCHASING
AND SUPPLY
CREST FLORAL STUDIO
DAVID ROBERTS FOOD CORPORATION
EAST PORT MFG.
EXECUTIVE FURNITURE GARAGE SALE
FREDA'S
GEORGE BOND SPORTS WAREHOUSE SALE
GIANT XMAS WAREHOUSE SALE
GIFTS THAT MAKE A DIFFERENCE
ICE CREAM WAREHOUSE SALE
JOTANI SPORTSWEAR - CATALOGUE OUTLET
SALE
LANCE LORENTS LIMITED
LCBO CLEARANCE CENTRE
LIZ CLAIBORNE SAMPLE SALE/DKNY JEANS
LYNN FACTORY OUTLET
MACDONALD FABER FABRICS
MARKHAM VITAMIN WAREHOUSE OUTLET -
NUTRITIONAL
PRODUCTS
MARKHAM WAREHOUSE OUTLET-NUTRITION-
AL PRODUCTS

MISSISSAUGA PARENTS OF MULTIPLE BIRTHS
ASSOCIATION
MOORE'S MEN'S WEAR
MUSKOKA LAKES WAREHOUSE SALE
NORAMA DESIGN WAREHOUSE SALE
NORTH YORK CENTENNIAL PRO SHOP SALE
NUTRITIONAL PRODUCTS
OLD FIREHALL SPORTS
PHANTOM WAREHOUSE SALE - CLEARANCE
OUTLET
PREMIER BRANDS WAREHOUSE SALE
PROCTOR & GAMBLE
REVLON WAREHOUSE SALE
RITCHÉ ANNUAL BRIDAL SALE
SCENTS ALIVE'S REAL FACTORY OUTLET SALE
SEW RIGHT - MASTER RIGHTS FACTORY
SALE
SNUG AS A BUG
STOLLERY'S
SWISS PEAK OUTLET SALE
THE BACK DOOR SALE
THE COMEBACK
THE FERN GROUP WAREHOUSE SALE
THE FINNISH PLACE
TWICE IS NICE
WARDEN POWER CENTRE DESIGNER SAMPLE
SALE
WAREHOUSE BOOK SALE
WESTPOINT STEVENS FACTORY OUTLET SALE
WORLD OF GIFTS AND HOME DÉCOR
ZACKS – FASHION OUTLET

T.B.A. TO BE ANNOUNCED - DATES NOT
AVAILABLE AT PRESS TIME

 THIS SYMBOL INDICATES WARE-
HOUSE SALES

index

Notes